Getting Started with Oracle Tuxedo

A practical guide to client/server technology using Tuxedo and extending it to SOA and cloud quickly

Biru Chattopadhayay

[PACKT] enterprise
PUBLISHING
professional expertise distilled

BIRMINGHAM - MUMBAI

Getting Started with Oracle Tuxedo

First published: June 2013

Production Reference: 1280513

Published by Packt Publishing Ltd.
Livery Place
35 Livery Street
Birmingham B3 2PB, UK.

ISBN 978-1-84968-688-4

www.packtpub.com

Credits

Author
Biru Chattopadhayay

Reviewers
Ransford Hewitt

Aivars Kalvans

Acquisition Editor
Rukhsana Khambatta

Commissioning Editor
Meeta Rajani

Technical Editor
Hardik B. Soni

Copy Editor
Aditya Nair

Project Coordinator
Michelle Quadros

Proofreader
Paul Hindle

Indexer
Tejal R. Soni

Graphics
Ronak Dhruv

Production Coordinator
Prachali Bhiwandkar

Cover Work
Prachali Bhiwandkar

Cover Image
Valentina Dsilva

About the Author

Biru Chattopadhayay has more than 20 years of international and diverse IT experience with a strong technical background and deep understanding of the relationship between technology and strategic business interests. He is of that rare breed of individuals who are very creative and who excel in highly technical assignments as well as in leadership roles. He has worked for product companies in the US and held senior positions in multinationals, where he has provided consulting and delivered solutions for various organizations around the world. He has been working with middleware since the early stages of his career and has a commanding knowledge of middleware, enterprise application integration (EAI), and SOA. Biru has worked for some of the best companies in the industry, such as BEA, Oracle, Tech Mahindra, and Dell. He has spoken in various international technical conferences on middleware, SOA, and e2e solutions.

I would like to thank my parents, Late Asha and Bhabani Chattopadhayay, for their blessings and for what I am today. My children, Bodhit and Ishani, for their effervescent curiosity as an added motivation, and most importantly my wife Kakoli for her unconditional support and encouragement.

About the Reviewers

Ransford Hewitt has over 10 years of experience in the design and development of distributed systems, and specializes in designing and troubleshooting large, high-performance, mission-critical systems built with various middleware technologies. Prior to joining Rogers Communications Partnership, Ransford spent two years as a system integrator, deploying the Amdocs Customer Care and Billing application mostly to large telecommunication companies, and spent another 18 years working with Cable & Wireless specializing in deploying and troubleshooting large, high-speed data communication systems. Ransford is currently a technical manager at Rogers Communications Partnership.

Aivars Kalvans holds the position of Lead Software Architect at Tieto Latvia and is working on the Card Suite payment-card system. Card Suite provides solutions for every single part of the payment-card business — issuing, acquiring, switching and clearing POI management, fraud and dispute management, and u-commerce.

During his career of more than 10 years, Aivars has been involved in a number of projects related to credit card issuing and acquiring utility payments through mobile phones, ATMs, and POS terminals. Aivars has been using Oracle Tuxedo (formerly BEA Tuxedo) since Version 8 in 2003. He enjoys solving both design and technical problems, and likes to work on personal and open source projects in his free time.

Aivars holds a Bachelor's degree in Computer Science from Riga Technical University and a Software Architecture Professional Certificate from the Carnegie Mellon Software Engineering Institute.

> I would like to thank my lovely wife Anete and sons Kārlis and Gustavs for making life much more interesting.

www.PacktPub.com

Support files, eBooks, discount offers and more

You might want to visit www.PacktPub.com for support files and downloads related to your book.

Did you know that Packt offers eBook versions of every book published, with PDF and ePub files available? You can upgrade to the eBook version at www.PacktPub.com and as a print book customer, you are entitled to a discount on the eBook copy. Get in touch with us at service@packtpub.com for more details.

At www.PacktPub.com, you can also read a collection of free technical articles, sign up for a range of free newsletters and receive exclusive discounts and offers on Packt books and eBooks.

http://PacktLib.PacktPub.com

Do you need instant solutions to your IT questions? PacktLib is Packt's online digital book library. Here, you can access, read and search across Packt's entire library of books.

Why Subscribe?

- Fully searchable across every book published by Packt
- Copy and paste, print and bookmark content
- On demand and accessible via web browser

Free Access for Packt account holders

If you have an account with Packt at www.PacktPub.com, you can use this to access PacktLib today and view nine entirely free books. Simply use your login credentials for immediate access.

Table of Contents

Preface

The client/server architecture is versatile and has a modular infrastructure. This technology is described as a cost-reduction technology. It includes fourth-generation languages, relational databases, distributed computing, and much more. Furthermore, it's been there for decades now; we can easily say that it's been there for multiple generations since the 80s. This book has been designed to give a quick reference to Tuxedo and the client/server architecture. Many books have been written on this technology, but this is the first book that bridges the gap between previous generations and the future generation. As I said, the client/server architecture, or Tuxedo, has been around for the past few decades now, and it is expanding every day! Today when we talk about Service Oriented Architecture (SOA) or Service Component Architecture (SCA), they are basically seen as new approaches to the client/server architecture. In this book, we are using our good old friend Tuxedo as a client/server platform, and we will learn how to build a distributed application using Tuxedo. What is the functionality of the Tuxedo components and the various APIs/parameters for development and configuration that make the Tuxedo-based applications so scalable, reliable, and highly-available in nature? Another question can be asked too, that is, is this Tuxedo still relevant for our current IT scenarios? The answer is obvious; it can be extended to the SOA world very easily, and you can call a Tuxedo service as a component of a composite when you are building an SCA-based application. Today, Tuxedo leverages one of the most futuristic machines, called Exalogic; it is easy to use and still gives you better ROI. In this book, there are some simple examples to explain the subject matter in an easier and practical way. Tuxedo has numerous out-of-the-box features and various ways to implement them to get best out of it; we have discussed as much as possible to give you the overall picture of how to build Tuxedo-based application leveraging these features.

Your feedback is very valuable to us. You can contribute by reporting any errors you find in the book, making suggestions for new content that you'd like to see in future updates, and by commenting and blogging about it.

What this book covers

Chapter 1, Getting Started with Tuxedo, introduces you to the distributed client/server technology using Tuxedo and tells you how it has evolved over the past decades. You will get an overview of the Tuxedo architecture and it's various important components and their functionalities. It also discusses various Tuxedo installation procedures, hardware and software requirements, and guidelines.

Chapter 2, Configuration and Administration of Tuxedo, guides you on how to configure a Tuxedo application and all its parameters with their syntax and relevant values. It covers the various Tuxedo administrative tools that are very important for a Tuxedo administrator to perform his/her daily work, and finally wraps up with tuning suggestions.

Chapter 3, Development of Tuxedo – Various APIs, discusses how to use Tuxedo APIs to build your applications, which are the clients combined with the server modules. Their syntax and value range has been provided as applicable. Also, it briefly describes all the Tuxedo buffer types, communication paradigms, and, most importantly, transactions processing (XA).

Chapter 4, Service Architecture Leveraging Tuxedo, covers SALT; this is an add-on product that allows external web service applications to invoke Tuxedo services and vice versa. It covers the basics of SALT and how to use SALT to connect a Tuxedo service from or to an SOA environment.

Chapter 5, Oracle Tuxedo Joining the Exalogic Family, discusses the Exalogic machine and its architecture briefly, and then discusses how to configure and deploy the Tuxedo application in this environment.

What you need for this book

You may need to download Tuxedo and SALT from the Oracle site at the following URL:

```
http://www.oracle.com/technetwork/middleware/tuxedo/downloads/
index.html
```

Please make sure you download the right version of Tuxedo for your specific operating system.

Who this book is for

This book is for anyone who wants to learn the client/server architecture using Tuxedo. It has been written in such a way that anyone who has a minimal knowledge of the client/server architecture can understand it and build the fundamental knowledge of Tuxedo and its APIs, commands, various important parameters, configuration file, and administrative tools. This book can be very helpful for architects, designers, developers, and administrators as a quick reference guide or as a guideline on how to build a Tuxedo application. The primary objective of this book is to show you how to develop distributed systems using Tuxedo and extend that to an SOA environment. It also gives the fundamentals of the Exalogic machines and how the Tuxedo application can leverage these new high-end machines for enterprise needs.

This book also helps business users to understand this technology, its various features and functionalities, and the related business benefits.

Many people in the IT field are not familiar with the general concept of the client/server technology, so a short overview of this is included in the introductory chapter.

Conventions

In this book, you will find a number of styles of text that distinguish between different kinds of information. Here are some examples of these styles, and an explanation of their meaning.

Code words in text, database table names, folder names, filenames, file extensions, pathnames, dummy URLs, user input, and Twitter handles are shown as follows: "You need to run wsdlcvt on the WSDL to produce a WSDF file."

A block of code is set as follows:

```
char *carrayPtr;
long carraysize;
. . .
carraysize = 1024;
carrayPtr = tpalloc ("CARRAY", NULL, carraysize);
```

When we wish to draw your attention to a particular part of a code block, the relevant lines or items are set in bold:

```
char *carrayPtr;
long carraysize;
. . .
carraysize = 1024;
carrayPtr = tpalloc ("CARRAY", NULL, carraysize);
```

Any command-line input or output is written as follows:

```
buildserver [-C] [-M] [-s services[:func[()]]] [-v] [-o outfile] [-f
firstfiles] [-l lastfiles] [{-r|-g} rmname] [{-r|-g} rmid:rmname] [-E
envlabel] [-t]
```

New terms and **important words** are shown in bold. Words that you see on the screen, in menus or dialog boxes for example, appear in the text like this: "Click on **NEXT** to proceed with the installation."

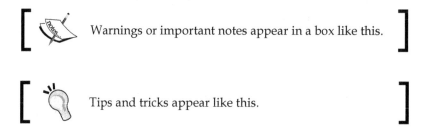

Warnings or important notes appear in a box like this.

Tips and tricks appear like this.

Reader feedback

Feedback from our readers is always welcome. Let us know what you think about this book—what you liked or may have disliked. Reader feedback is important for us to develop titles that you really get the most out of.

To send us general feedback, simply send an e-mail to feedback@packtpub.com, and mention the book title through the subject of your message.

If there is a topic that you have expertise in and you are interested in either writing or contributing to a book, see our author guide on www.packtpub.com/authors.

Customer support

Now that you are the proud owner of a Packt book, we have a number of things to help you to get the most from your purchase.

Errata

Although we have taken every care to ensure the accuracy of our content, mistakes do happen. If you find a mistake in one of our books—maybe a mistake in the text or the code—we would be grateful if you would report this to us. By doing so, you can save other readers from frustration and help us improve subsequent versions of this book. If you find any errata, please report them by visiting http://www.packtpub. com/submit-errata, selecting your book, clicking on the **errata submission form** link, and entering the details of your errata. Once your errata are verified, your submission will be accepted and the errata will be uploaded on our website, or added to any list of existing errata, under the Errata section of that title. Any existing errata can be viewed by selecting your title from http://www.packtpub.com/support.

Piracy

Piracy of copyrighted material on the Internet is an ongoing problem across all media. At Packt, we take the protection of our copyright and licenses very seriously. If you come across any illegal copies of our works, in any form, on the Internet, please provide us with the location address or website name immediately so that we can pursue a remedy.

Please contact us at copyright@packtpub.com with a link to the suspected pirated material.

We appreciate your help in protecting our authors, and our ability to bring you valuable content.

Questions

You can contact us at questions@packtpub.com if you are having a problem with any aspect of the book, and we will do our best to address it.

1
Getting Started with Tuxedo

In this introductory chapter, we'll discuss Oracle Tuxedo for distributed client/server technology and how it has evolved over the past decades. It gives you a comprehensive overview of Tuxedo architecture and its various important components and their functionalities. It then follows with Tuxedo installation procedures in brief and hardware and software requirement guidelines.

Introduction to the distributed client/server architecture using Tuxedo

Tuxedo is a middleware for building multitier client/server applications in heterogeneous distributed environments. It stands for Transactions under UniX Extended for Distributed Operation (TUXEDO). It is also called the Transaction Monitoring (TP Monitor) system. Tuxedo has been around for more than three decades now and it is expanding every day. Today, the Service Oriented Architecture (SOA) or Service Component Architecture (SCA) is considered as the new architectural approach, but Tuxedo has been based on this approach from the beginning. Tuxedo has been used to build various mission-critical distributed applications around the world that are extremely scalable, reliable, and highly available in nature. One may question whether Tuxedo is still relevant in the current IT scenarios? The answer is YES! It can easily be extended to an SOA environment, where the Tuxedo service can be called as a component of a composite in SCA-based applications. The latest Tuxedo can run on an **Exalogic** machine, one of most futuristic machines for cloud computing. All these features are very natural to the Tuxedo environment and returns better ROI.

In Tuxedo, a client program acts like a consumer who initiates a call to the service or a server, which is the provider for the service. The service is always in a ready state to accept a request from the client.

Some of the basic features of Tuxedo in the distributed client/server model are as follows:

- The server and the client are functional modules with distinct interfaces. The APIs are standards-based (SCA, XATMI, and CORBA). The functions performed by a client and a server can be implemented by a set of software modules run on the same or different machines.

- Each client/server association is established between two functional components when a client component initiates a service request for a server, which responds to the service request.

- Transaction management is one of the most important features of Tuxedo; for example, two-phase commit protocol, which is also known as XA.

- Tuxedo provides a reliable message queuing mechanism called **/Q**, which supports XA. It provides a reliable and persistent queuing technique that allows applications to unequivocally queue requests to a queue.

- The following additional features, although not required, are typical of the client/server model:

    ○ There are various types of message-passing mechanisms, which are typically asynchronous, synchronous, unsolicited notification, conversational, or publish/subscribe.

    ○ Clients and servers typically reside on separate machines connected through a network, but they can reside in the same machine too.

- There are various security features such as auditing, authorization, authentication, and encryption available for use.

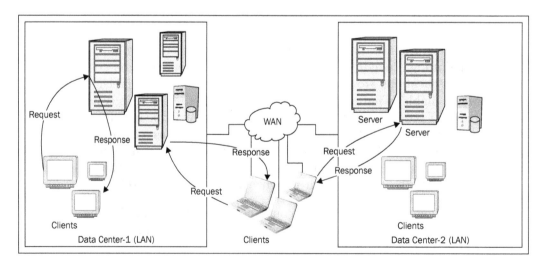

Some of the benefits of client/server technology

The advantages or benefits of a clean client/server model are manifold; some of them are as follows:

- **Modular application design** – Divides application processing across multiple machines, with the following conditions:
    - ° Non-critical data and functions are processed on the client
    - ° Critical functions are processed on the server

- **Optimization** – Optimizes the server for data processing and storage (for example, large computers and disk space)

- **Reduced network traffic** – Due to the three-tier architecture, data doesn't need to travel back and forth from frontend clients to databases multiple times

- **Scales horizontally** – Multiple servers, each having capabilities and processing power, can be added to distribute processing load

- **Scales vertically** – Can be moved to more powerful machines, such as a minicomputer or a mainframe, to take advantage of the larger system's performance

- **Reduces data duplication** – Data is stored on the servers instead of clients, reducing the amount of data replication for the application

The history of Tuxedo

Tuxedo was developed by Bell Labs in 1983 to achieve multiuser access and manipulate a database on a mainframe computer simultaneously. In 1989, the Unix System Laboratories (USL) promoted Tuxedo as a client/server framework and launched this product. In 1993, Novell acquired USL and Tuxedo became Novell's product. In 1996, BEA bought the rights for Tuxedo from Novell. Tuxedo did wonders for many Fortune 500 companies around the world. In 2008, Tuxedo became an Oracle product along with all the other BEA Systems products, for example, WebLogic server, and others.

Tuxedo architecture and anatomy

Clients and servers are the application-processing components of a Tuxedo system. Server processes provide one or more named services. Client processes can request services without having to know where they are located. The named service feature provides a directory of services that result in the request being routed to one of the servers providing the service. Clients and servers communicate by sending messages. When the clients and servers are distributed over different machines, Tuxedo makes the networking infrastructure by connecting the client and server machines, while keeping the client/server request-response model transparent. Programmers therefore do not have to worry about where the service is located or what the underlying network protocols are. The application's code remains the same whether the clients and servers are running on a single machine or distributed over multiple machines.

The basic middleware characteristics that Tuxedo supports are as follows:

- Simplifies the segregation of the clients' and servers' logic.

- Manages and helps in monitoring distributed transactions among multiple data sources.

- Extremely modular in nature; one or more servers may fail without affecting the applications running on the same Tuxedo environment.

- Communicates with heterogeneous databases using various resource managers within a single application for transactional integrity.

- Integrity of the code and data for a server are centrally maintained, making it is easy to maintain and protect data integrity. This supports the horizontal and vertical scalability of applications. Horizontal scaling is adding or removing of hardware with only a small performance effect. Vertical scaling is moving to a bigger and faster server or adding servers.

- Supports service-requests prioritization, load balancing, data-dependent routing, and queuing.

- The clients and servers are loosely coupled processes that can exchange service requests and replies using messages.

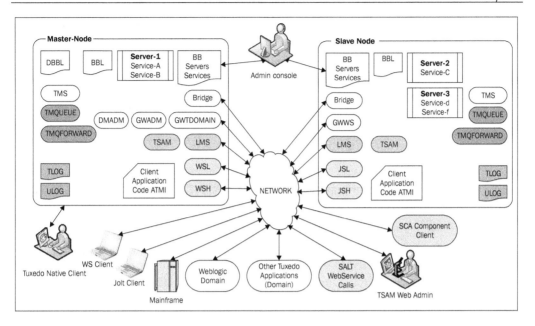

Tuxedo has a very rich set of internal components (shown in the previous diagram) that provide runtime support for application availability, scalability, and extendibility. I will briefly introduce them to you in this chapter and we will be discussing them in detail in the following chapters; they are as follows:

- **Bulletin Board** (**BB**): This is the first process as you start Tuxedo; it stores the configuration and dynamic information for the whole Tuxedo system. It stays in the shared memory and is available to all the processes of the Tuxedo system. The BB translates a service name to a specific server. When a client calls a service, the BB is used to look up which servers offer the requested service, and based on this information, the request message is put on the request queue of the correct server. Once the message is ready to be passed on to the client, it enqueues it to reply queue for the designated client.

- **Bulletin Board Liaison** (**BBL**): This Tuxedo administrative process monitors the other processes of Tuxedo systems.

- **Distinguished BBL**: The DBBL is the master monitor for a multimode (clustered) Tuxedo environment, responsible for overseeing the BB on each node. Also, for networked applications, a backup node may be designated for the DBBL.

- **Bridge**: This process is used for multinode (MP mode) configurations, which are responsible for inter-node communications in networked applications.

- **TMS**: This is the transaction manager server dedicated to a particular resource when distributed transaction processing is employed.

- **Master machine/node**: In a multiple machine configuration (clustered), the Tuxedo domain that holds the UBBCONFIG file is called the master machine. All the administering tasks, such as starting, stopping, and monitoring, can be done from this server in a Tuxedo domain.

- **Tuxedo server processes**: These are the executable programs that offer named services through the Tuxedo system. They are normally customer-developed programs. One server (program/executable) may contain one or more service (functions) in it.

- **Tuxedo client processes**: These are executable programs that call services through the Tuxedo system. They are usually customer-developed programs.

- **Workstation Listener (WSL)**: This is the Tuxedo server process that works as a listener for the WS client (workstation). As a handshaking process, this server listens to the WS clients and assigns connections to a WS Handler (another Tuxedo-provided server) accordingly for the rest of the correspondence with the WS client until it disconnects from a Tuxedo instance. The WSL manages the pool of WS Handler processes and the demands by starting and stopping them in response to the load.

- **Workstation Handler (WSH)**: This is another process provided by Tuxedo that works in conjunction with WSL. This gateway process handles communications between WS clients and the Tuxedo server application. This WSH handles multiple WS clients within the same Tuxedo domain. A WSH works like a multiplexer to accommodate all the requests and replies with a particular WS client over a single connection.

- **Jolt Listener/Handler (JSL/JSH)**: These are Tuxedo listening and gateway processes for Java-based workstation clients; they are similar to WSL/WSH in terms of functionality.

- **TMQUEUE**: This message-queuing manager is a Tuxedo-system-supplied server that enqueues and dequeues messages on behalf of programs.

- **TMQFORWARD**: This message-forwarding server is a Tuxedo-system-supplied server that forwards messages from a queue to other servers.

- **DMADM**: This is one of the three servers provided by Tuxedo for using the Tuxedo domain configuration. This is an administrative server that provides a registration service for gateway groups. The DMADM server works with other domain gateway admin servers (GWADM); during the initialization process, it registers the configuration information that is mandatory for the requesting gateway group. The DMADM server preserves all the names of registered gateway groups, and it also proliferates changes to these groups as they are made in the domain configuration file (BDMCONFIG). We will discuss domain configuration in *Chapter 3*, *Development of Tuxedo – Various APIs*.

- **GWADM**: This Tuxedo system gateway admin server registers with the DMADM server to get the configuration data used by the other gateway group. This server accepts requests from the domain admin server for runtime information or changes occurred during runtime for a gateway group.

- **GWTDOMAIN**: This Tuxedo system server is called Domain Gateways, and it is very asynchronous in nature. It has the multi-tasking functionality and can handle outgoing and incoming service requests to or from other remote domains.

- **LMS**: The Local Monitor Server (LMS) is a Tuxedo system server. A LMS is required on each Tuxedo machine if the node needs to be monitored; we will discuss this in detail in *Chapter 2*, *Configuration and Administration of Tuxedo*, under *Tuxedo System and Application Monitoring* (*TSAM*).

- **GWWS**: This is a Tuxedo system server and a major component for **Service Architecture Leveraging Tuxedo** (**SALT**). It works like a bidirectional (inbound and outbound) adapter that connects with other web service applications using SOAP over HTTP/S protocols.

- **Connecting WebLogic Domain**: The WebLogic Tuxedo connector is an add-on product that works as a bidirectional adapter for Tuxedo services and WebLogic server applications. The adapter helps the WebLogic server's clients to call a Tuxedo service and Tuxedo clients to call any WebLogic server's Enterprise Java Beans (EJBs).

In this section, we introduced Tuxedo's client/server concepts in brief, its overall architecture, and its various important components. We will discuss them in detail in the following chapters to understand their functionalities and usage patterns. In the following section, we will see how to install Tuxedo and also see what the post-installation tasks are that you must carry out to make sure the installation is successful. The installation of Tuxedo is very simple even though it supports a wide variety of operating systems and hardware. We will focus on the basic installation procedure and its guidelines, which covers your primary requirement of installing Tuxedo.

Installation of Tuxedo

As mentioned before, Tuxedo supports various OSs and hardware; you need to make sure you get the right installable file.

Hardware and software requirements

The Oracle Tuxedo software needs to be installed on each server that will run the Tuxedo application, or can be called Tuxedo domain.

- x86 or x86-64 – This denotes various CPUs based on x86 or x86-64 architecture. Most of the current platforms are supported; the following are the most common ones:
  - ° HP 11i (32-bit/64-bit)
  - ° IBM AIX 5.3 (32-bit/64-bit)
  - ° IBM AIX 6.1 (32-bit/64-bit)
  - ° MS Windows 7 (32-bit)
  - ° MS Windows 2008 server (32-bit/64-bit)
  - ° Oracle Enterprise Linux 5.0 (32-bit/64-bit)
  - ° Oracle Solaris 10 (32-bit /64-bit) on x86-64
  - ° Red Hat Linux Enterprise AS 5 (32-bit) on x86

- Memory requirements – The following are the minimum memory requirements recommended by Oracle to run your application:
  - ° 1 GB of RAM
  - ° 4 MB of RAM for each Oracle Tuxedo system server

- Hard disk – The following is the minimum hard disk requirement recommended by Oracle:
  - ° 2 GB of disk space is required for Tuxedo installation

> Note that the Oracle Tuxedo installation program creates a temporary directory to extract the files from the archive prior to installing Tuxedo on the target system. So, it is important to have sufficient space during installation. The JRE is moved to the Oracle home directory from the temporary file at the end of the installation process.

For more details on hardware and operating systems, Oracle Tuxedo's support policy, or more related information, please refer to the following link:

```
http://docs.oracle.com/cd/E26665_01/tuxedo/docs11gr1/install/inspds.
html
```

Platform-specific installer files for the Oracle Tuxedo product software are available for download at Oracle's corporate website:

```
http://www.oracle.com/technetwork/middleware/tuxedo/downloads/index.
html
```

Tuxedo installation components

You can start your installation once you have downloaded the installation file, but it is good to know that there are seven installation sets bundled in Tuxedo, and you can choose any one of them during installation. They are listed as follows:

- Full: All components of the Oracle Tuxedo 11*g* Release, that is, the server and client components
- Server: The server components of Tuxedo
- Full client: The client components of Tuxedo
- ATMI (/WS) client: The workstation component of Tuxedo
- CORBA client: The C++ client and SSL components of Tuxedo
- Jolt client: The Java client (Jolt) components of Tuxedo
- .NET client: The .NET version of the workstation client components of Tuxedo

 The Oracle home directory is where all the common files (executable and internal files) that are accessed by other Oracle components (residing on the same machine) are stored. It is very important to keep in mind that the home directory is important for ensuring that the Oracle software behaves correctly. During the installation, you are asked for this home directory. According to best practices, you need to have one home directory, though you may choose to have multiple in a system.

Installation procedures

The Oracle Tuxedo can be installed in three different ways; we will briefly go through each of them in the following sections.

Graphical user interface (GUI) installation

The graphical user interface installation is the GUI-based Oracle Tuxedo installation program that runs on Unix- and Windows-based systems. This is the most popular way to install Tuxedo.

The following are the steps to be followed for a GUI-mode installation on a Windows system:

1. Log in to the Windows system as an administrator (preferred), as you need admin privileges to install Oracle Tuxedo server components on a Windows system. To install Tuxedo client components, you do not need to be logged in as an administrator.

2. To install Oracle Tuxedo, click on the installer file to start the installation.

3. Continue running the GUI-mode installation process.

4. Log in to the system again after the Tuxedo installation is completed.

The following are the steps for a GUI-mode installation on a Unix system:

1. You need to log in as the Oracle Tuxedo administrator.

2. You need to go to the directory where you downloaded the installer and run the installation program, as shown in the following sample command:

    ```
    UnixPrompt> sh filename.bin
    ```

    Here, `filename` is the name of the Oracle Tuxedo installer file.

 You will get an error message and the installation process will fail if the GUI interface in your system is not available. In this case, you may want to use the silent or console-mode installation.

Console installation

The console installation is a text-based installation that is only available for Unix systems.

1. You need to log in as the Oracle Tuxedo administrator.

2. You need to go to the directory where you downloaded the installer and run the installation program, as shown in the following sample command:

   ```
   UNIXprompt> sh filename.bin -i console
   ```

   Here, `filename` is the name of the Oracle Tuxedo installer file.

3. To complete the installation, follow these steps:

   1. Enter the number of your choice or press *Enter* to accept the default.

   2. Enter `back` or `previous` at the prompt to review or change your selection.

   3. Enter `quit` in response to any prompt to exit the installation process.

 Oracle strongly recommends Unix users to create a separate user account for the Oracle Tuxedo administrator and have the ownership of the Oracle Tuxedo files for that account.

Silent installation

The silent installation is a more automated way of installing Tuxedo. This installation reads the strings from a text file that you can create prior to beginning the installation. This can be used as the standardized installation for all installations in the enterprise in such a way that you set the installation configurations only once and use it multiple times. You need to create a properties file for the installer; for detailed step-by-step instructions, please go to the following link:

```
http://docs.oracle.com/cd/E26665_01/tuxedo/docs11gr1/install/inssil.
html
```

As we are done with the installation (by either of the three processes), it is recommended to verify the Tuxedo ATMI software installation by running `simpapp`. The sample applications are installed during the Tuxedo installation. You can find this simple application under your Tuxedo directory; `\samples\atmi\simpapp`. There is a `README` file in the same directory for a walkthrough.

Summary

In this chapter, we introduced Tuxedo as a client/server platform where you can build your distributed application, and its benefits. We also discussed Tuxedo architecture and how it has evolved over the past years. We briefly discussed the various components of Tuxedo, and finally saw how to install Tuxedo in various modes for different operating systems. I have mentioned some of the important guidelines and prerequisites to help you set up the environment for your Tuxedo installation. The installation is very interactive and simple, so I have not put in any screenshots or line-by-line instructions.

2
Configuration and Administration of Tuxedo

In this chapter, we will discuss the essentials of Tuxedo configuration and administration and the tools used by a Tuxedo administrator to perform day-to-day operations.

In this chapter, we will cover the following topics:

- Administration of a Tuxedo application
- Structure of a Tuxedo application (configuration file)
- Parameters in the configuration file
- Environment variables
- Commands and tools to build, monitor, and change the Tuxedo system configuration
- Various important components and built-in features of Tuxedo
- Tuning and monitoring guidelines

This chapter is basically dedicated to Tuxedo administrators and is divided into two main categories. The first one is configuring and setting up a Tuxedo application, and the other is monitoring/administrating a Tuxedo application. It is very important to understand how to structure a Tuxedo application using a configuration file called UBBCONFIG, as well as to understand each and every parameter in the configuration file, their dependency and hierarchy, and the environment variables. For monitoring purposes, we need to know the various commands and tools, how to change the Tuxedo system configuration at runtime, and how to tune various parameters for higher throughput. At the end of the chapter, I will share some tuning/monitoring guidelines, which may help you to get the best out of a Tuxedo application.

Tuxedo administration

In this section, we will discuss the elements of the Tuxedo administration, such as the role of an administrator, how to configure and structure a Tuxedo application, various useful commands, how to manage or monitor a Tuxedo application, some important built-in features of Tuxedo, components such as queue and domain, and tuning guidelines.

Responsibility of a Tuxedo administrator

The Tuxedo administrator needs to play a central coordinating role by working closely with application designers, operating system administrators, network administrators, and database administrators to ensure end-to-end management of the Tuxedo application, which is distributed in nature. The primary responsibilities of a Tuxedo administrator are configuring, managing, and monitoring the Tuxedo application. The most important one for a Tuxedo administrator is how to plan, execute, and maximize the use of computing resources. He/she also needs to use various administrative tools in a centralized manner, just like a cockpit for his/her enterprise, and perform proactive actions to keep the Tuxedo application available in the most efficient manner. Tuxedo administrators need to know the status of a machine, network failures, database system failures, and other problems that have a global impact on the operation of an application.

Some important tasks of an administrator are as follows:

- **Installation**: Installing the software and verifying it to make sure that the software is installed properly and the integrity of the directory structure is maintained as per the recommendation

- **Ensuring that all machines are properly tuned**: It is very important to have OS-level parameters tuned as per Oracle Tuxedo's recommendation so that the Tuxedo application runs optimally

- **Designing and organizing**: Designing and organizing an application built on Tuxedo in such a way that all the components of the application (workstations, servers, resource managers, and system resources) work as expected

- **Deployment architecture**: The administrator needs to have a clear footprint of the Tuxedo components and how all the applications are deployed in the platform as well as their relationships and dependencies

- **Monitoring the application**: This is the most important task that needs to be done 24/7; alert messages should be implemented in such a way that he/she can be proactive and detect issues before they interfere with business

- **Security**: A strong security module needs to be in place to ensure that the application (services) is used in a proper manner; no one other than the administrator should be able to change anything in the system

- **Diagnosing and rectifying Tuxedo issues**: He/she should diagnose problems occurring in the operation of the application and then take corrective action

- **Upgrade plan**: This could be upgrading Tuxedo or the OS patch; he/she needs to plan accordingly to ensure that the system downtime is minimal and does not affect the flow of business

- **Governance module**: Implementing a strong governance module to ensure that all the applications getting deployed on the Tuxedo platform meet quality standards, thus maintaining the stability and scalability of the applications

Configuring and setting up a Tuxedo application

Under this section, we will discuss how a Tuxedo application is structured and configured using the UBBCONFIG file as well as the associated environment variables to set up the environment before you use Tuxedo.

Environment variables

There are various environment variables that need to be properly set so that the Tuxedo application works in the expected manner.

Variables for the Tuxedo application/server node are as follows:

- TUXDIR – This is the directory where your Tuxedo is installed

- TUXCONFIG – This is the full path where you have the TUXCONFIG file

- PATH – This is the directory path for the Tuxedo binary application that has to be added in the PATH variable (for example, $TUXDIR/bin:Application Directory:$PATH)

The following are the environment variables if you use the VIEW/VIEW32 buffer:

- VIEWFILES – The name of the VIEW/VIEW32 file; a comma-separated list if you have multiple files

- VIEWDIR – The application directory where you have the VIEW/VIEW32 file; a colon-separated list of the VIEW/VIEW32 file directories

The following are the environment variables if you use the FML/FML32 buffer:

- FIELDTBLS – The name of the FML file; a comma-separated list of files in case you have multiple files

- FLDTBLDIR – The application directory where you have the FML file; a colon-separated list of the FML file directories

- FIELDTBLS32 – The name of the FML32 file; a comma-separated list of files in case you have multiple files

- FLDTBLDIR32 – The application directory where you have the FML32 file; a colon-separated list of the FML file directories

In Unix, the LD_LIBRARY_PATH variable is used to load the libraries dynamically in the memory as you run the application. This variable is called differently in various versions of Unix and even Microsoft operating systems; please make sure you are using the proper name, as follows:

```
LD_LIBRARY_PATH = $TUXDIR/lib
```

For the queue, the QMCONFIG variable must contain the full pathname of the file or raw device that will contain the queue device; see the following example:

```
QMCONFIG = Full path of the queue file/device
```

Configuring and structuring a Tuxedo application

The Tuxedo configuration file, also called the UBBCONFIG file, is the most important configuration file for a Tuxedo environment or application. The UBBCONFIG file is a text file that contains various sections to structure your application, and each section has parameters with respective values to configure and manage the Tuxedo application. It has eight sections, of which five sections are required for all configurations: RESOURCES, MACHINES, GROUPS, SERVERS, and SERVICES; the rest of the sections (NETGROUPS, NETWORK, and ROUTING) are optional. This is a text file, so it can be created or maintained using any text editor that works with a text file.

Let's see an example of the UBBCONFIG file to show the overall structure of a Tuxedo application.

The following UBBCONFIG file shows the two-machine (MP mode) configuration along with the most important parameters. I have added the NETWORK and ROUTING sections to give you a real-life example:

```
*RESOURCE
IPCKEY      80952 # key for well known address
DOMAINID    My_Domain
UID         0777  # use it for inter process communication
GID         007   # use it for inter process communication
PERM        0707  # Access permissions for inter process
                    communication
MAXSERVERS  40    # Number simultaneous servers
MAXSERVICES 50    # Number of services can be publish within same
                    domain
MAXGTT      25    # Number of simultaneous global transactions
MASTER      SITE1
SCANUNIT    10
SANITYSCAN  12
BBLQUERY    180
BLOCKTIME   30
OPTIONS     LAN,MIGRATE
MODE        MP  # single or Multi node configuration
LDBAL       Y   # To set the load balancing

#
*MACHINES
machUnix LMID=SITE1 TUXDIR="/usr/tuxbin"
        MAXACCESSERS=20
        APPDIR="/usr/Biru/apps/MyApps"
        ENVFILE="/usr/Biru/apps/MyApps/ENVFILE"
        TLOGDEVICE="/usr/Biru/apps/MyApps/TLOG"
        TLOGNAME=TLOG
        TUXCONFIG="/usr/Biru/apps/MyApps/tuxconfig"
        ULOGPFX="/usr/Biru/apps/MyApps/ULOG"

machNT   LMID=SITE2 TUXDIR="C:\Biru\apps\MyApps\tuxbin"
        MAXACCESSERS=20
        MAXWSCLIENTS=25
        APPDIR="C:\Biru\apps\MyApps"
        ENVFILE="C:\Biru\apps\MyApps\ENVFILE"
        TLOGDEVICE="C:\Biru\apps\MyApps\TLOG"
        TLOGNAME=TLOG
        TUXCONFIG="C:\Biru\apps\MyApps\TLOG\tuxconfig"
```

```
            ULOGPFX="C:\Biru\apps\MyApps\TLOG\ULOG"
#
*GROUPS

Branch1     LMID=SITE1   GRPNO=11
Branch2     LMID=SITE2   GRPNO=21


#
*NETWORK
SITE1      NADDR="machUnix.80952" BRIDGE="/dev/starlan"
           NLSADDR="machUnix.serve"
#
SITE2      NADDR="machNT.80952"
           NLSADDR="machNT.serve"


*SERVERS
#
DEFAULT: RESTART=Y MAXGEN=5 REPLYQ=Y CLOPT="-A"

Teller    SRVGRP=Branch1   SRVID=11
Account   SRVGRP=Branch1   SRVID=12
Balance   SRVGRP=Branch1   SRVID=13

Teller    SRVGRP=Branch2   SRVID=21
Account   SRVGRP=Branch2   SRVID=22
Balance   SRVGRP=Branch2   SRVID=23

*SERVICES
DEFAULT:     LOAD=50      AUTOTRAN=N
WITHDRAWAL   PRIO=50      ROUTING=ACCOUNT_ID
DEPOSIT      PRIO=50      ROUTING=ACCOUNT_ID
CLOSE_ACCT   PRIO=40      ROUTING=ACCOUNT_ID
OPEN_ACCT    PRIO=40      ROUTING=BRANCH_ID
ABAL         PRIO=30      ROUTING=b_id
TBAL         PRIO=30      ROUTING=b_id
#
*ROUTING
ACCOUNT_ID   FIELD=Bank_ACCOUNT_ID  BUFTYPE="FML"
             RANGES="MIN - 9999:*,100-599:Branch1,600-
                     9999:Branch2,*:*"
BRANCH_ID    FIELD=Bank_BRANCH_ID    BUFTYPE="FML"
             RANGES="MIN - 999:*,1-499:Branch1,500-999:Branch2,*:*"
b_id         FIELD=b_id  BUFTYPE="VIEW:aud"
             RANGES="MIN - 0:*,1-5:BA Branch1,6-10: Branch2,*:*"
```

The following diagram depicts the relationship between the sections within the UBBCONFIG file mentioned previously:

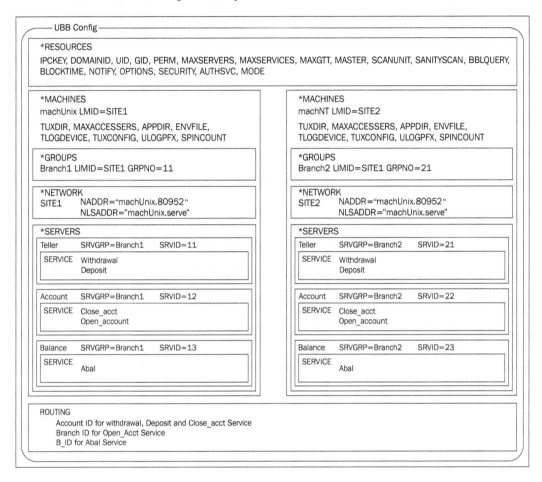

We will now discuss all the important parameters in brief for each of the eight sections of the UBBCONFIG file.

The RESOURCES section

This section contains information pertaining to all the resources in the domain; for example, the number of servers and services under the SERVICE section.

Parameter name and values	Required/ optional	Comments/values – what it means
IPCKEY = numeric_value	Required	This is the unique address of the inter-process communication (IPC) resources. It is also used to derive a number of other addresses (for example, the name of BB in a multimode system).
UID = numeric_value GID = numeric_value	Optional	This is the security access for a Tuxedo application – the user ID (UID) / Group ID (GID) of the administrator. The default is the user ID of the user who runs tmloadcf.
MAXACCESSERS = numeric_value	Optional	The maximum number of processes that can concurrently be attached to a Bulletin Board (BB), which includes clients and system-supplied as well as application servers where the administrative processes are not counted.
MAXSERVERS = numeric_value	Optional	The number of servers in a domain; the MAXSERVERS value can range from 0 to 8,192; the default value is 50.
MAXSERVICES = numeric_value	Optional	The number of services in a domain; the MAXSERVICES value can range from 1 to 8,192; the default value is 100.
MAXINTERFACES = numeric_value	Optional	The maximum permissible number of CORBA interfaces.
MAXOBJECTS = numeric_value	Optional	The maximum permissible number of CORBA objects.
SCANUNIT = numeric_value	Optional	This defines the time interval (seconds). You can set the number of times the BBL will periodically check the sanity of servers local to its machine. In addition, you can set the number of timeout periods for blocking messages and transactions.

Parameter name and values	Required/ optional	Comments/values – what it means
DBBLWAIT = numeric_ value	Optional	In the MP mode configuration, the DBBL waits for the reply/response from BBL in (SCANUNIT * DBBLWAIT) seconds, and the timeout occurs accordingly.
BBLQUERY = numeric_ value	Optional	This is the heartbeat interval used by DBBL to check the health of all the BBLs, so the product of BBLQUERY and SCANUNIT is the interval time.
MASTER = String1 [,String2]	Required	Here, String1 is the master machine's name and String2 is the backup master machine's name.
MODEL = {SHM | MP}	Required	This indicates the type of system; SHM means a single node and MP means multiple nodes in the system.
SECURITY = {NONE | APP_PW | USER_AUTH | ACL | MANDATORY_ACL}	Optional	This is to set the security feature for an application; NONE means default will be used.
DOMAINID = String	Optional	This is the name of the domain; it sets to null if you do not input anything.
LDBAL = {Y | N}	Optional	To turn off and turn on the load balancing. TMNETLOAD can be used for local preference.
MAXBUFTYPE = numeric_ value	Optional	The maximum number of buffer types and subtypes.
MAXCONV = numeric_ value	Optional	The maximum number of conversations allowed on a machine.
MAXNETGROUPS = numeric_value	Optional	The highest number of network groups that can be defined under the NETWORK section.
BLOCKTIME = numeric_ value	Optional	This is the multiplier of SCANUNIT and BLOCKTIME, which is to set the time out for a blocking call; it must be more than zero.

The **MACHINES** section

The MACHINES section is where you define the logical names for a physical machine's configuration. All parameters need to specify a specific machine. In this section, you need to define all the parameters for all the physical machine(s) for an application under the same Tuxedo domain.

Parameter name and values	Required/ optional	Comments/values – what it means
NETLOAD = number	Optional	This is used to control the communication between the local server and the remote server. The load is the extra cost to go to the remote server over the network.
LMID = String	Required	The logical name(s) of the physical machine(s).
SPINCOUNT = number	Optional	The number of attempts to lock the Bulletin Board at the user level before blocking calls.
TYPE = String	Optional	This is to group the same type of machines; for example, data encoding/decoding can be avoided between the same type of machines during communication.
TUXCONFIG = String	Required	The complete pathname of the TUXCONFIG file.
TLOGSIZE = numeric (size in page)	Optional	The size of the transaction log.
ENVFILE = String	Optional	This is used to set the environment for the clients or servers on any particular machine from a named file. If the value specifies an invalid filename, no values are added to the environment.
TLOGDEVICE = String	Optional	The name of the device or file where the transaction log (TLOG) for this application resides.
TLOGNAME = string_vlue	Optional	You can specify the name of the transaction logfile; Tuxedo uses TLOG as the default name.

Parameter name and values	Required/ optional	Comments/values – what it means
MAXACCESSERS = number	Optional	The maximum number of processes (including clients and servers) that can be concurrently associated with the Bulletin Board. This should be more than 0 but less than 32,768.
MAXOBJECTS = number	Optional	This is specifically for a CORBA-based application to specify the number of CORBA objects that can be simultaneously housed in the Active Object table.
MAXGTT = number	Optional	The highest permissible number of concurrent transactions (global) in a particular domain.
MAXWSCLIENTS = number	Optional	This is to specify the number of accessed entries on a machine to be reserved for /WS or SALT clients.
GID = number UID = number	Optional	This is the group ID and user ID to be associated with the IPC structures created for the Bulletin Board.
TUXDIR = String	Required	The absolute pathname of the Tuxedo installation.
APPDIR = String	Required	One or more absolute pathnames (colon-separated list) to specify all the application and administrative servers booted within the same environment.
CMPLIMIT = number	Optional	This is the threshold message size for the messages; automatic data compression will be performed beyond this value.
ULOGPFX = String	Optional	The pathname for the user's logfile on a machine.

The GROUPS section

The GROUPS section helps to specify a logical name for a group of the same type of servers and/or services within a machine. At least one server group needs to be defined in this section.

Parameter name and values	Required/ optional	Comments/values – what it means
GROUPNAME = string_ value	Required	This specifies the logical name of a group; the maximum value can be 30 characters long.
GRPNO = number	Required	This is the number associated with a server group and it needs to be unique; the value can range from 1 to 30,000.
CLOSEINFO = string_ value	Optional	This is used to close the resource manager.
OPENINFO = string_value	Optional	This is used to open the resource manager.
ENVFILE = string_value	Optional	The environment under which all the servers in the group are to be executed; this environment is specified in the named file.
LMID = string_value1 [, string_value2]	Required	This maps the servers for one or multiple machines; refer to the previous section, *The MACHINES section*.
TMSNAME = string_value	Optional	This is to map a transaction manager server with a group.
TMSCOUNT = number	Optional	This is to specify the instances of transaction manager servers to begin with for a group, and to automatically set up in an MSSQ.

The NETWORK section

In the NETWORK section, you need to configure a network for a LAN environment for communication between the Tuxedo application and the various domain nodes.

Parameter name and values	Required/optional	Comments/values – what it means
BRIDGE = String	Optional	The BRIDGE parameter uses this device on the same LMID value to access the network.
NADDR = String	Required	This is the network ID / hostname of a machine and port number for a BRIDGE process, which is the listener process within the same LMID value. For example, //host.name:port_number.
MINENCRYPTBITS = {0 | 40 | 56 | 128}	Optional	The minimum level of encryption that is required when the network link is established.
MAXENCRYPTBITS = {0 | 40 | 56 | 128}	Optional	The maximum level of encryption that is required when the network link is established.
NETGROUP = String	Optional	The network group related with this network entry.
NLSADDR = String	Optional	The network and port to define the tlisten process. For example, //#.#.#.#:port.

The SERVER section

The SERVER section provides information on the initial conditions for servers started in the system. This is an executable program created by buildserver; so as a process, this executable continually runs and waits for service requests.

Parameter name and values	Required/optional	Comments/values -- what it means
CONV = {Y | N}	Optional	This is used to configure the server as a conversational server.
SEQUENCE = number	Optional	The sequence of a server: when it should boot up or shut down relative to other servers.
MIN = number	Optional	The minimum number of instances of the server to be booted by tmboot.

Parameter name and values	Required/ optional	Comments/values -- what it means
MAX = number	Optional	The maximum number of instances of the server that can be booted.
CLOPT = String	Optional	During boot up, the servopts options can be conceded to a server process. So, this is a string of command-line options that are passed to the Tuxedo servers when they are booted.
ENVFILE = String	Optional	You may use this to set more environment variables for a server during its initialization.
SRVGRP = String	Required	The logical name related to a server group in the GROUPS section.
SRVID = number	Required	This unique number is used to classify a server within a group.
RQADDR = String	Optional	This is the name of the request queue for the server.
RQPERM = number	Optional	The numeric representation of permissions for the request queue; by default, it is 0666.
REPLYQ = {Y | N}	Optional	This is to say if we can have a reply queue for the process or not.
MAXGEN = number	Optional	This is to restart the server the specified number of times.
GRACE = number	Optional	This is the interval in seconds for restarting the server.
RESTART = {Y | N}	Optional	This is to turn off or turn on the option of restarting for a server.

The SERVICE section

The SERVICE section provides information on services used by an application. Tuxedo does not require listing services in this section. It is best practice for an administrator to list all the services here for future reference or ease of maintenance.

Parameter name and values	Required/ optional	Comments/values -- what it means
AUTOTRAN = {Y | N}	Optional	This is used to automatically turn the transaction on if the request is not part of a transaction.
BUFTYPE = "type1[:subtype1 [,subtype2 . . .]] [;type2[:subtype3[, . . .]]] . . . "	Optional	The types of data buffers used for this service.
LOAD = number	Optional	This is to weigh the service with a number proportionate to its load on the system. This is used for tuning purposes; the higher the number, the higher the load.
ROUTING = String	Optional	The name of the routing criteria used for this service when data-dependent routing is used. If this parameter is not specified, data-dependent routing is not done for this service. A string must be 15 characters or less in length. If multiple entries exist for the same service name but with different SRVGRP parameters, the ROUTING parameter must be the same for all of these entries.
SRVGRP = String	Optional	The name of the server group from which SVCNAM gets all the group parameter settings.
PRIO = number	Optional	The dequeuing priority of **SVCNM**.
BLOCKTIME = number	Optional	This sets the non-transactional blocking time value, in seconds, of the indicated service.
SVCTIMEOUT = number	Optional	The amount of time, in seconds, that is allowed for the processing of the indicated service. The value must be greater than or equal to zero. A value of zero indicates that the service will not be timed out.
TRANTIME = number	Optional	This is the default timeout value, in seconds, for a transaction automatically started for the associated service. The default is 30 seconds. A value of zero implies that no timeout occurs for the machine.

The ROUTING section

The ROUTING section provides information for data-dependent routing of service requests using Tuxedo buffer types such as the FML, VIEW, and XML buffers.

Parameter name and values	Required/ optional	Comments/values -- what it means
ROUTING_CRITERIA_NAME = string_value	Required	This is a name assigned to a routing parameter for a service defined in the SERVICE section.
FIELD = string_value	Required	This is the actual routing based on the values of the field from the FML or FML32 buffer, XML element or the element attribute, or the VIEW or VIEW32 field name.
FIELDTYPE = string_value	Required	The type of routing field specified in the FIELD parameter, which can be one of CHAR, SHORT, LONG, FLOAT, DOUBLE, or STRING.
RANGES = string_value	Required	A range is either a single value or a range of the lower-upper form.
BUFTYPE = string_value	Optional	This can be one of FML, FML32, XML, VIEW, VIEW32, X_C_TYPE, or X_COMMON. No subtype can be specified for types FML, FML32, or XML.

The NETGROUPS section

The NETGROUPS section describes the network groups available to the application in a LAN environment. There are only three parameters in this group: NETGROUP is the name of the network group, while NETGRPNO and NETPRIO with numeric values are used to specify the priority of this network group.

Parameter name and values	Required/ optional	Comments/values -- what it means
NADDR = String	Required	This specifies the network address (as its listening address) for the BRIDGE process under LMID, so that other BRIDGE processes are contacted through this address within the same application. For example, //host.name:port_number.

Parameter name and values	Required/ optional	Comments/values -- what it means
BRIDGE = String	Optional	The device name to be used by the BRIDGE process placed on that LMID to access the network.
FADDR = String	Optional	This is to specify the network address used by one machine connecting to other machines. This parameter, along with the FRANGE parameter, determines the range of the TCP/IP ports to which a process will attempt to bind before making an outbound connection.
FRANGE = number	Optional	This is to specify the range of TCP/IP ports to which a native process will attempt to bind before making an outbound connection. The FADDR parameter specifies the base address of the range.
NETGROUP = String	Optional	String is the network group associated with this network entry. If unspecified, the default, DEFAULTNET, is assumed. The NETGROUP parameter, if not set to DEFAULTNET, must have previously appeared as a group name in the NETGROUPS section of the file.

Things to remember

The following are the things to remember when configuring and structuring a Tuxedo application:

- Once you have your UBBCONFIG file, you need to run the tmloadcf command to create the TUXCONFIG file, which is a binary version of UBBCONFIG. As with UBBCONFIG, the TUXCONFIG file may be given any name (for example, tmloadcf -y ubbconfig).

- The TUXCONFIG environment variable defines the location on the master machine where the tmboot command uses the binary TUXCONFIG file, so it must be set to an absolute pathname ending with the device or the system file where TUXCONFIG is to be loaded.

- In a multimachine Tuxedo domain running different releases of the Tuxedo system software, the master machine must run the latest release of the Tuxedo system software in the domain.

- The master machine for a Tuxedo domain contains the master copy of the TUXCONFIG file, which gets propagated to all the other server machines as you run tmboot to boot the application.

In the previous section, we have discussed the various environment variables that need to be set in the Tuxedo application, and we have also described all the sections and parameters of the UBBCONFIG file to set up your Tuxedo application, which is the most important file for a Tuxedo application.

Tuxedo commands

There are a huge number (around 100) of commands with various options to administrate a Tuxedo system. I have listed all the commands in this section and picked up the most important ones to discuss in brief.

The buildclient command

This is used to construct a Tuxedo ATMI client module; its syntax is as follows:

```
buildclient [-v] [{-r rmname | -w }][ -o name]  [ -f firstfiles] [ -l lastfiles]
```

Let's discuss the attributes of this command:

- -v: The buildclient command should work in verbose mode to ensure that all the messages can be seen during compilation.

- -r: This option specifies the resource manager associated with this client to be part of a transaction.

- -w: This option specifies that the client is to be built using the workstation libraries; native mode is default.

- -o: This option specifies the filename of the output load module. If not supplied, the load module is named a.out.

- -f: This option specifies one or more user files to be included first in the compilation and link edit phases of buildclient, before the Oracle Tuxedo ATMI libraries.

- -l: This option specifies one or more user files to be included last in the compilation and link edit phases of buildclient, after the Oracle Tuxedo ATMI libraries.

The buildserver command

This command constructs the Tuxedo ATMI server module. Its syntax is as follows:

```
buildserver [-C] [-M] [-s services[:func[()]]][-v] [-o outfile] [-f
firstfiles] [-l lastfiles] [{-r|-g} rmname] [{-r|-g} rmid:rmname] [-E
envlabel] [-t]
```

Let's discuss the attributes of this command:

- -C: This option stipulates the COBOL compilation.
- -M: This option specifies the server to be associated with multiple XA-complaint resource managers; this option is mandatory.
- -s: The names of services that can be advertised when the server is booted.
- -v: The buildserver command should work in verbose mode to ensure that all messages can be seen during compilation.
- -o: This option specifies the filename of the output load module. If not supplied, the load module is named SERVER.
- -f: This option specifies one or more user files to be included first in the compilation and link edit phases of buildserver, before the Oracle Tuxedo ATMI libraries.
- -l: This option specifies one or more files to be included last in the compilation and link edit phases of buildserver, after the Oracle Tuxedo ATMI libraries.
- -r: This option specifies the resource manager associated with this server.

The buildtms command

This command is used to construct a transaction manager server module. When integrating a new resource manager into the Tuxedo system, the $TUXDIR/udataobj/RM file must be updated to include the information about the resource manager. The format of this file is as follows:

```
rm_name:rm_structure_name:library_names
```

The following is the syntax of the buildtms command:

```
buildtms [ -v ] -o name -r rm_name
```

Let's discuss the attributes of this command:

- -v: The buildtms command should work in verbose mode
- -o: This option specifies the name of the output file
- -r: The resource manager associated with this server; the value rm_name must appear in the resource manager, as previously mentioned

The tmloadcf command

This command is used to convert the text version of the UBBCONFIG file to its equivalent binary configuration to boot the Tuxedo application. It reads the UBBCONFIG file and checks the syntax. If the SECURITY parameter is specified in the RESOURCES section of the UBBCONFIG file, tmloadcf will ask for the application password as you run it. The following is the syntax of this command:

```
tmloadcf  [-n] [-y] [-c] [-b blocks] {UBBCONFIG_file | -}
```

Let's discuss the attributes of this command:

- -n: This option is used for checking the syntax of the UBBCONFIG file without updating the TUXCONFIG file.
- -y: This option is used for prompting on the console.
- -c: This option is used to calculate and display the minimum IPC resources needed for this configuration.
- -b: This option specifies the block size for the device. It is a recommended option if you are using a raw device. You may ignore it if the filesystem already exists.

The tmboot command

The tmboot command brings up the Tuxedo application instance. This can be invoked by the Tuxedo administrator to bring up the Tuxedo application in whole or in a part by using the following parameters:

```
tmboot [-l lmid] [-g grpname] [-i srvid] [-s aout] [-o sequence]
[-S] [-A] [-b] [-B lmid] [-e command] [-w] [-y] [-g]
[-n] [-c] [-m] [-M] [-dl]
```

Let's discuss the attributes of this command:

- -l lmid: All the groups associated with this LMID value will boot and all associated TMSs and gateway servers will also boot accordingly.
- -g grpname: The same as above for group names mentioned by grpname.
- -s server name: All servers in the SERVERS section are executed by server name.
- -o sequence: All servers with the sequence parameter are executed.
- -S: All servers in the SERVERS section are executed.

- -A: All administrative servers for machines in the MACHINES section are executed. Use this option to guarantee that the DBBL, all BBLs, and the BRIDGE processes are brought up in the correct order.

- -b: Boot the system from the BACKUP node (without making this machine the master).

- -B lmid: A BBL is started on a processor with the logical name lmid.

- -m 1-n: Temporarily resets the runtime MIN values for servers specified with the -s option with a common MIN value.

- -M: This is used to boot all the administrative processes on the master machine.

- -dl: This is used to display on the standard output; it is very useful when you use sdb to debug application services.

- -e command: This option causes the command to be executed if any process fails to boot successfully.

- -w: This option should be used with caution. It informs tmboot to boot another server without waiting for servers to complete initialization.

- -y: This option means that you need to boot all the administrative and server processes.

- -q: This option suppresses the printing of the execution sequence on the standard output. It implies -y.

- -n: The execution sequence is printed but not performed.

- -c: The minimum IPC resources needed for this configuration are printed.

The tmshutdown command

This command shuts down a set of Tuxedo servers. Only the Tuxedo application administrator can run this command. It can only be invoked from the master machine. It also shuts down the entire server if no other parameter is passed.

```
tmshutdown [options]
```

List of Tuxedo commands

The following is the list of Tuxedo commands:

- buildwsh: This command builds a customized workstation handler process

- buildclient: This command compiles and builds a Tuxedo client module

- `buildclt`: This command compiles and builds a Tuxedo workstation client program on the MS platform
- `buildserver`: This command compiles and builds a Tuxedo server
- `buildtms`: This command compiles and builds a TMS load module
- `buildwsh`: This command compiles and builds a customized workstation handler process
- `cobcc`: This command is the COBOL compilation interface
- `dmadmin`: This is the administration command interpreter for Tuxedo domains
- `dmunloadcf`: This command unloads a `BDMCONFIG` file (a binary domain configuration file)
- `gencat`: This command generates a formatted message catalog
- `mkfldhdr`/`mkfldhdr32`: This command creates FML/FML32 header files from field tables
- `mklanginfo`: This command compiles language-information constants for a locale
- `qmadmin`: This is an administration command interpreter for the queue manager
- `rex`: This command is an offline regular expression, compiler, and tester
- `tidl`: This is an Interface Definition Language compiler
- `tlisten`: This is a generic listener process
- `tmadmin`: This is the command interpreter for Tuxedo Bulletin Boards
- `tmboot`: This command brings up a Tuxedo configuration
- `tmconfig`: This command dynamically updates and retrieves information about a running Tuxedo application as either a native client or a workstation client
- `tmipcrm`: This command removes IPC resources allocated by a Tuxedo application on a local machine
- `tmloadcf`: This command parses a `UBBCONFIG` file (a text-format configuration file) and loads a `TUXCONFIG` file
- `tmshutdown`: This command shuts down a set of Tuxedo servers
- `tmunloadcf`: This command unloads a `TUXCONFIG` file (a binary configuration file)

- `tpacladd`: This command adds a new access control list entry on the system
- `tpaclcvt`: This command converts Tuxedo's security data files
- `tpacldel`: This command deletes an access control list entry
- `tpaclmod`: This command modifies an access control list entry on the system
- `tpadduser`: This command creates a Tuxedo password file
- `tpdelusr`: This command deletes a user from a Tuxedo password file
- `tpgrpadd`: This command adds a new group to the system
- `tpgrpdel`: This command deletes a group from the system
- `tpmodusr`: This command maintains a Tuxedo system password file
- `tpusradd`: This command adds a new principal to the system
- `tpusrdel`: This command deletes a user from the system
- `tpusrmod`: This command modifies user information on the system
- `tuxadm`: This is the CGI gateway for the Tuxedo Web GUI
- `tuxwsvr`: This is the mini web server for use with the Tuxedo Web GUI
- `txrpt`: This is the Tuxedo system's server/service report program
- `ud`, `wud`, and `/ud32/wud32`: These are Tuxedo's universal client programs
- `uuidgen`: This command generates a Universal Unique Identifier (UUID)
- `viewc` and `viewc32`: These commands view the (data) compiler for Tuxedo
- `viewsviewdis` and `viewdis32`: These commands view the disassembler for binary view files
- `wlisten`: This is the Tuxedo Web GUI listener process

For detailed options on all these Tuxedo commands, please refer to the following URL:

```
http://docs.oracle.com/cd/E26665_01/tuxedo/docs11gr1/rfcm/rfcmd.
html#wp1330814
```

Monitoring and changing a Tuxedo application

The administrator needs to be able to constantly monitor and tune parameters, add or remove a user, deploy or undeploy an application, and create or change queues, access control lists, and so on. The Tuxedo MIB contains all the information needed for the operation of an Oracle Tuxedo application. There are two different administrative tools that access the MIB and allow for dynamic configuration of a Tuxedo application. The third one is the Tuxedo Admin Console, which has not been updated since Tuxedo 8, and hence it is not included in our discussion.

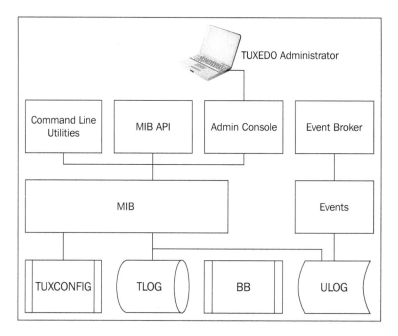

The following is a list of the MIB's components:

- **WS_MIB**: For workstation groups and the processes associated with them
- **ACL_MIB**: For administrating access control lists
- **APPQ_MIB**: For administrating queues
- **EVENT_MIB**: For event notification and the subscription request database
- **DM_MIB**: For administrating the Tuxedo domains' (multiple-domain) configurations

The command-line interface

This is a set of commands used to manage, activate, configure, and deactivate the application (for example, tmadmin, and so on). Each of these commands have various options to get administrative information or control.

The tmadmin() command provides 51 interactive commands that allow the administrator to monitor a Tuxedo application's performance, reconfigure, troubleshoot, or take corrective actions. Normally, it runs on an active node; for an inactive application, it can only be run on the master node.

tmadmin [-r] [-c] [-v]

The following are the attributes of this command:

- -r: This invokes tmadmin as a client (read-only) instead of as the administrator
- -c: This invokes tmadmin in the configuration mode.
- -v: This invokes tmadmin to display the Tuxedo version number and license number

Once tmadmin has been invoked, commands can be entered at the prompt (>). Some of the most important of the 51 commands are mentioned in the following list:

- bbclean machine: It removes a hanged server process and the resources associated with it. It also reboots the process if it is configured as restartable. It also makes the DBBL check the status of the BBL(s).
- bbparms: It gives you a summary of the Bulletin Board's parameters; for example, the maximum number of servers, objects, interfaces, and services.
- help [{command | all}]: This provides help for all commands; if a command is specified, the abbreviation, arguments, and description for that command are printed.
- master [-yes]: This command is run on the master node when the backup node is acting as the master. It migrates the DBBL to the master node; the backup node is no longer acting as the master node.
- printqueue [qaddress]: This gives you the queue information for all the application and administrative servers; qaddress can be used to restrict information to a specific queue.
- printserver [-m machine] [-g groupname[-R rmid]] [-i srvid] [-q qaddress]: This command gives information about the application or administrative server. Various options can be used to filter the server information.

`tmconfig()` allows the administrator to examine and modify the TUXCONFIG files for the Tuxedo application. These changes are dynamic in nature, as changes made to the TUXCONFIG file are propagated to all machines under the same application as soon as possible. Most of the parameters can be modified in TUXCONFIG and can take immediate effect dynamically, without rebooting the application.

1. When you run `tmconfig`, it prompts for the desired section.

   ```
   %promt%> Section: 1) RESOURCES, 2) MACHINES, 3) GROUPS 4) SERVERS
   5) SERVICES 6) NETWORK 7) ROUTING q) QUIT 9) WSL 10) NETGROUPS 11)
   NETMAPS 12) INTERFACES [1]:
   ```

2. It then prompts for the desired operation.

   ```
   %promt%> Operation: 1) FIRST 2) NEXT 3) RETRIEVE 4) ADD 5) UPDATE
   6) CLEAR BUFFER 7) QUIT [1]:
   ```

3. It then prompts you to indicate whether or not you want to edit the input buffer.

   ```
   %promt%> Enter editor to add/modify fields [n]?
   ```

   ```
   %promt%> Enter editor to correct?
   ```

4. Finally, `tmconfig` asks whether the operation should be performed.

   ```
   %promt%> Perform operation [y]?
   ```

Performing the preceding steps gives you the return value after completion of the job.

If you decide to quit the application and select an option, it prompts you to create a backup text version of the configuration (as you may have changed the configuration file).

```
%promt%> Unload TUXCONFIG file into ASCII backup [y]?
```

If you select a backup, `tmconfig` prompts for a filename.

```
%promt%> Backup filename [UBBCONFIG]?
```

It indicates that a backup was created successfully, otherwise, an error is printed.

The Tuxedo MIB application programming interface

We have discussed how to use the GUI and command-line interfaces for monitoring the Tuxedo applications, but you can also write a program using a Management Information Base (MIB) interface for monitoring purposes that can modify the TUXCONFIG file for you if you need to make changes to any configuration. The MIBs provide the framework for programmed administration of the Tuxedo system. For more information, please refer to Oracle online documentation.

Tuxedo System and Application Monitoring (TSAM)

TSAM is an Oracle Tuxedo add-on product that provides comprehensive monitoring and reporting for the Tuxedo application. It monitors runtime performance bottlenecks and business-data fluctuations, determines service models, and provides notification when predefined thresholds are violated. In this section, we will discuss and provide an overview on its architectural components and the relation between them, the installation procedure, and a quick start guideline to monitor your Tuxedo application using TSAM. TSAM comprises of the following two components:

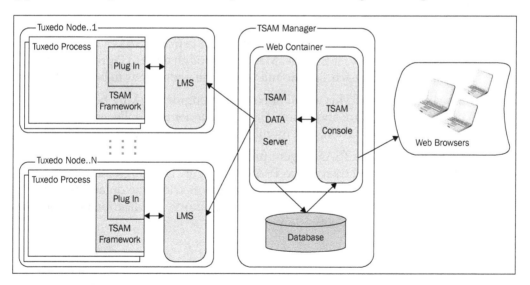

TSAM Manager runs on a Java application server; for example, the Oracle WebLogic server and Apache Tomcat. It provides a graphical user interface to correlate and aggregate performance metrics collected from one or more Tuxedo domains and then displays it in real time.

TSAM Manager also has two major components:

- **Oracle TSAM Data Server** is the communication interface to TSAM. It accepts requests from a Local Monitor Server (LMS) and metrics-query requests from the web browser. It also does the following tasks:
    - Accepting data from the LMS and storing them into the database
    - Accepting requests from the representation layer and data processing
    - Communicating with the LMS for configuration instructions

- **Oracle TSAM Console** is the web application that provides a GUI for administration and data presentation. After logging on to the TSAM Console, you have access to all the TSAM functionalities.

The TSAM Agent collects various performance metrics for applications, including XA and non-XA transactions, services, and system servers. The TSAM Agent handles all the Tuxedo-side backend logic. It works in conjunction with the TSAM Manager. The TSAM Agent must be installed on top of Tuxedo. It has three components, as follows:

- **Local Monitor Server (LMS)**: The LMS is a Tuxedo system server (that needs to be configured in UBBCONFIG) that gets the data from TSAM's default plugin and passes the data to the TSAM Manager through an HTTP protocol. The LMS is required on each Tuxedo machine if the node needs to be monitored.

- **TSAM Framework**: This is a data-collection engine working between the Tuxedo infrastructure and other TSAM components. It collects the runtime metrics, alerts evaluation, and monitors policy enforcement.

- **TSAM Plug In**: The TSAM Agent provides default plugins for sending data to the LMS and then to the TSAM Manager. The plugin allows custom plugins to be hooked to intercept the metrics. The default plugin communicates with the LMS with shared memory. Applications will not be blocked at the metrics-collection point.

Installing TSAM

TSAM can be installed basically in two modes: GUI mode in Unix or Windows, and console mode for Unix machines. We will be using the console-mode installation in this book. GUI-mode installation is very self-explanatory, and it goes through the same steps as console installation, so please refer to the following instructions for GUI installation too.

The following steps are required to install the TSAM Manager and the TSAM Agent software in console mode on a certified Unix platform. Please read the prompt carefully, as these displays are very interactive and you need to give the input accordingly. You may go through the following 11 steps and write down your input before you start your installation. It is also a good idea to look at steps 1 and 2 under the *Using TSAM for monitoring – quick path* section to ensure that you understand how TSAM works and the components you will need and how to deploy them. Otherwise, you may need to do lot of manual work even when there are lots of scripts provided to you for ease of use. I am giving you the following step-by-step displays, but there could be a little variation between this and the one on the screen, so please be careful:

1. Execute the installation program, which launches the installation script.

   ```
   # sh <installer_name> -i console
   ```

   The following is the installation script:

   ```
   Preparing to install...
   Extracting the JRE from the installer archive...
   Unpacking the JRE...
   Extracting the installation resources from the installer
   archive...
   Configuring the installer for this system's environment...
   ```

2. Press the *Enter* key to continue.

3. The next screen prompts you to choose the Oracle TSAM 11*g* Release 1 (11.1.1.2.0) install set.

   ```
   Choose Install Set
   ------------------
   Please Choose the Install Set to be installed by this installer.
       1- Full Install
       2- Agent Install
       3- Manager Install
   ENTER THE NUMBER FOR THE INSTALL SET OR PRESS <ENTER> TO ACCEPT
   THE DEFAULT (Full Install):
   ```

4. The next screen prompts you to choose the Oracle home directory.

   ```
   Oracle Home Directory Selection
   -------------------------
       1- Choose existing Oracle Home directory
       2- Specify Oracle Home directory
   ```

If you select 2, you must specify an Oracle home directory. The path of this directory must be an absolute existing pathname with write permission, otherwise the following message is displayed:

```
--------------------------------------------------
Overwrite feature?
The following TSAM 11gR1 feature is found under
/apps/OracleHomes/tsam11gR1
...
Do you want to overwrite it?
1- No
2- Yes
```

5. Modify or change the default Oracle TSAM Manager installation folder.

```
Choose Install Folder
1- Modify Current Selection (/apps/OracleHomes/tsam11gR1)
2- Use Current Selection (/apps/OracleHomes/tsam11gR1)
ENTER AN ABSOLUTE PATH, OR PRESS <ENTER> TO ACCEPT THE DEFAULT:
```

6. Choose the authentication type. If you choose the Full or Manager install set, the **Choose Authentication Type** screen appears as follows:

```
Choose Authentication Type
--------------------------
User information can be stored in the Oracle TSAM database or an
existing LDAP server.
The authentication type "Local first" supports both.
"LDAP only" exclusively supports LDAP authentication.
        1- Local first
        2- LDAP only
ENTER THE NUMBER FOR YOUR CHOICE, OR PRESS <ENTER> TO ACCEPT THE
DEFAULT:
```

If you choose Local first, the installer prompts the following:

```
--------------------------
Do you want to specify an LDAP configuration file now?
1- No
Yes
```

If you choose `No`, you can specify the LDAP configuration file by running the LDAP deployment utility, **LDAPDeployer**, after installation.

Note that if you choose `No` in this process, there is no LDAP configuration file deployed. You must deploy an LDAP configuration file manually after installation by using the LDAP deployment utility (`LDAPDeployer.sh` or `LDAPDeployer.cmd`) if you want to enable LDAP authentication. For more information, see the *Deploying Oracle TSAM Manager in the Oracle TSAM Deployment* guide.

If you choose `LDAP only` as the authentication type, or `Yes`, you must input the path of the LDAP configuration file, as follows:

```
---------------------------
Enter an existing LDAP configuration file:
```

7. Specify the database type; if you choose the `Full` or `Manager` install set, the **Choose Database Type** screen appears as follows:

```
Choose the TSAM Manager database type you want to install:

------------------------

1- Bundled Derby database

2- An existing Derby database

3- An existing Oracle database

4- Skip, I will deploy TSAM 11gR1 to an existing database server
after the installation
```

8. Specify the database connection. If you choose to connect to an existing Derby or Oracle database, the **Specify Database Connection** screen appears as follows:

```
Specify the host name:

Specify the port:

Specify the database name:

Specify user name:

Specify the password:
```

If you choose to create a new database, Oracle TSAM 11*g* R1 creates a user with the name `admin`. You are prompted to specify and verify the password accordingly.

```
Enter the administrator group ID (DEFAULT: 0):

Enter the viewer group ID (DEFAULT: 1):
```

9. If the install mode `Full Install` or `Manager Install` is selected, you are prompted to choose an application server.

```
Choose an application server

-----------------------

1- Bundled Tomcat Server

2- An existing Tomcat Server

3- An existing WebLogic server

4- Skip, I will deploy TSAM 11gR1 to an existing application
server after the installation

If 1 is selected, Oracle TSAM startup/shutdown script/ and the
Oracle TSAM Manager war package is copied to Install Directory.

If 2 is selected, you are prompted to specify an existing Tomcat
folder. Enter an existing Tomcat folder.

If 3 is selected, you are prompted to specify an existing WebLogic
Server directory.

Oracle WebLogic Server directory selection

-----------------------

1- Choose an existing WebLogic Server directory

2- Specify an existing WebLogic Server directory
```

Note that if you select 4, Oracle TSAM Manager will not be deployed during installation. You must deploy it manually to an existing application server by using the application server utility (`AppServerDeployer.sh` or `AppServerDeployer.cmd`).

If you choose to deploy to an existing WebLogic server, you are required to input the following WebLogic server connection parameters:

```
Enter Oracle WebLogic admin url:

Enter Oracle WebLogic user name:

Enter Oracle WebLogic password:
```

The existing WebLogic server is expected to be located on the local installation machine. WebLogic servers that exist remotely are not supported.

10. Please review the preinstallation summary information printed on the screen; please make sure that you have the information you desired to have.

```
PRESS <ENTER> TO CONTINUE:
```

11. Once the installation is complete, the following message is displayed:

```
Installation Complete
---------------------
::

::

Congratulations….. installed to:
PRESS <ENTER> TO EXIT THE INSTALLER:
```

For a GUI-based installation, you need to run the Oracle TSAM installation program. It can run on both Windows and Unix systems. Once you launch the GUI, the inputs are the same as the current installation.

Various administrative tasks using TSAM

TSAM is a very useful tool for a Tuxedo administrator, as he/she can use it for many useful monitoring, tuning, or reporting tasks that he/she needs to perform daily to keep the Tuxedo system healthy:

- Tuxedo has several important system servers: BRIDGE, GWTDOMAIN, and GWWS. As you know, BRIDGE connects multiple Tuxedo machines within a Tuxedo domain. Similarly, GWTDOMAIN connects one Tuxedo domain with others and GWWS is the web service gateway for all the SALT components. The system server monitors and tracks message throughput, awaiting the reply messages on each network connection for BRIDGE and GWTDOMAIN. For GWWS, the web service requests statistics will be collected.

- There are various performance-related monitoring tasks; some of them are as follows:

    ○ **Service name**: The name of an Oracle Tuxedo service.

    ○ **Location**: The set of metrics to identify the process that sends the performance metrics. It includes information about the domain, machine, group and process names, and so on.

    ○ **IPC queue length**: The message number in an IPC queue.

    ○ **IPC queue ID**: The Oracle Tuxedo identifier of an IPC queue.

    ○ **Execution time**: The time spent in milliseconds for executing an Oracle Tuxedo service or an XA call.

- ° **Wait time**: The time taken by a message in the transportation stage.

- ° **CPU time**: The CPU time consumed by the service for processing the request. It only applies to single-threaded servers.

- ° **Message size**: The Oracle Tuxedo message size.

- ° **Execution status**: The `tpreturn` service-return code. It is defined by the Oracle Tuxedo ATMI interface.

- ° **Elapse time**: The time elapsed for a call is monitored.

- ° **Pending message number**: The number of pending messages to the network.

- ° **Message throughput**: The total number of messages and volume accumulated in the system server monitoring intervals.

- ° **Waiting reply message number**: The number of requests in `GWTDOMAIN` awaiting a reply from the remote domain.

- ° **J2EE-based solution**: This is a pure web-based solution with WEB 2.0 technologies; easy to deploy, configure, and use. The TSAM Console can be used from anywhere using any standard web browser.

- ° Easy-to-understand metrics database schema. The metrics can be used for data mining or further business analysis.

- TSAM helps analyze global distributed transactions and correlate transactions across multiple domains in the tree style. TSAM supports the transaction monitoring propagation; that is, if monitoring is enabled for the transaction initiator, the whole transaction path will be monitored.

- A powerful monitoring policy can help achieve the exact monitoring results while reducing the impact on performance. The sampling can be based on interval, ratio, and runtime data. The monitoring can be turned on or off dynamically without restarting the application.

- Comprehensive SLA alert configurations based on monitoring metrics. Alert evaluation is based on Tuxedo FML Boolean expressions. The event generated by alert can be posted to the Tuxedo Event Broker. Some alert types can also drop stale service requests.

- Programming APIs that retrieve the metadata packaged in a monitored call help developers make application decisions dynamically.

Using TSAM for monitoring – quick path

We have installed TSAM and gone through its monitoring capabilities. Now we will take a quick path to start monitoring an existing Tuxedo application using TSAM. The steps are described assuming that we have chosen all the default choices during installation (for example, the database, web server, and so on) to ensure that we do not need to do any manual deployment or configuration. Therefore, we will be using all automated scripts provided by TSAM to deploy and configure TSAM or the required components before we start monitoring. In the following examples, we will use Unix script; there are similar Windows script available for Windows. I have picked up WebLogic and an Oracle database, as these are the natural choices.

1. Deploy the Oracle TSAM Agent.

   You need to add the LMS to each `MACHINES` section of the `UBBCONFIG` file, as follows:

   ```
   *MACHINES
   Site1
   ...
   *GROUPS
   LMS-GRP LMID=Site1
   ...
   *SERVERS
   LMS    SRVGRP=LMS-GRP SRVID=1
     MINDISPATCHTHREADS=1
     MAXDISPATCHTHREADS=5
     CLOPT="-A -- -l tsamweb.abc.com:8080/tsam"
   ...
   ```

   The `-l` option specifies the Oracle TSAM Data Server address, which is configured in the Oracle TSAM Manager.

   Now, as normal procedure, you need to run `tmloadcf` on this new `UBBCONFIG` file and reboot the application.

2. Deploy the Oracle TSAM Manager:

   ° **Oracle TSAM Manager LDAP Deployment**: The TSAM Manager works as a web application in a servlet/JSP container. It uses the database to store persistent Tuxedo performance and monitoring data. Before using the Oracle TSAM Manager, it must be deployed to a database server and a web application container. If you have provided LDAP information during installation, the LDAP deployment is done automatically; otherwise, you must do the LDAP deployment using the `LDAPDeployer.sh/LDAPDeployer.cmd` utility, which you can find under the `deploy` directory under the TSAM installation folder, if you want to enable the LDAP authentication.

○ **Oracle TSAM Manager Database Server Deployment**: Also, if you select a database during installation, the Oracle TSAM Manager is deployed on the specified database server automatically; otherwise, you must deploy the Oracle TSAM Manager to a database server using the `DatabaseDeployer.sh/DatabaseDeployer.cmd` utility, which you can find under the `deploy` directory under the TSAM installation folder. For example, to deploy TSAM to an Oracle database with the user `Tuxedo` and the password `ADMIN` in Unix, do the following (use `.cmd` for Windows):

```
Prompt> cd < TSAM_DIR >/deploy
```

```
Prompt> ./ DatabaseDeployer.sh -type oracle -hostname
localhost -port 1521 -dbname TSAM -user Tuxedo -password
ADMIN -overwrite no -admingid 0 -viewergid 1 -adminpassword
admin1
```

For more information on deployment or manual deployment, please refer to `http://docs.oracle.com/cd/E26665_01/tsam/docs11gr1/deployment/deploy.html#wp1065923`.

○ **Oracle TSAM Application Server Deployment**: Oracle TSAM provides application server deployment utilities called `AppServerDeployer.sh/AppServerDeployer.cmd`, which help you to deploy it to an existing application server (WebLogic or Tomcat) automatically after installation; otherwise, you will have to do it manually.

For example, for deploying TSAM to a WebLogic server in Unix, do the following (use `.cmd` for Windows):

```
Prompt> cd < TSAM_DIR >/deploy
```

```
Prompt>./AppServerDeployer.sh -type weblogic -adminurl
localhost:7001 -directory /home/oracle/wlserver_10.3 -user
weblogic -password weblogic1
```

○ **Changing the configuration parameters**: The TSAM Manager can be run on Oracle WebLogic or the Apache Tomcat server without changing any configuration parameters.

On WebLogic, you can change `Listening Port`, `Session Timeout`, `HTTP KeepAlive`, `POST Maximum Byte Size`, `Maximum Thread Simultaneous Processing`, or `Maximum Incoming Connection Requests`, as required.

On a similar note, for the Apache Tomcat server, you can change `Minimum JAVA Option Memory Size`, `Listening Port`, `Session Timeout`, `HTTP KeepAlive`, `POST Maximum Byte Size`, `Maximum Thread Simultaneous Processing`, or `Maximum Incoming Connection Requests`, as required.

- **Starting up the Oracle TSAM Manager**: If you have chosen the bundled Apache Tomcat server and the bundled Derby database during installation, the startup/shutdown script files are installed in the Oracle TSAM `/bin` folder.

  For example, start the Oracle TSAM Manager in Unix as follows (use `.cmd` for Windows):

  ```
  Prompt> cd <TSAM_DIR>/bin
  Prompt> ./startup.sh
  ```

3. Find your Oracle Tuxedo configuration.

   Log in to the Oracle TSAM Manager Console (for example, `http://localhost:8080/tsam/faces`).

   In the console page, the user accessibility settings can be adjusted as follows:

   - **The login screen** – In the upper left-hand corner of the login screen, click on the **Settings** drop-down menu. You can select the following three options; the settings take effect immediately:

     - **I use a screen reader**: Accessibility specific constructs are added to improve the screen's reader behavior.

     - **I use high contrast colors**: The application's display uses high-contrast instead of the default contrast.

     - **I use large fonts**: The application's display uses large fonts instead of the default-size fonts.

   - **The console page** – In the upper right-hand corner of the Oracle TSAM Console page, click on **Accessibility**. The **Accessibility Preferences** page appears; it has the same three user accessibility options as the login screen.

     When you have selected your options, click on **OK**; the settings will take effect immediately.

     Your Oracle Tuxedo configuration information can be found in the Oracle Tuxedo component tree panel.

4. Configure the monitoring policy.

    TSAM provides comprehensive monitoring control of the Tuxedo infrastructure, and the monitoring policy defines what and how you want to monitor.

    On the menu bar, click on **Policy** and select **Tuxedo Application Runtime Monitoring Policy** from the drop-down menu. The **Monitoring Policy List** page appears. It displays the existing defined Tuxedo application runtime monitoring policies and allows you to view, add, edit, or delete policies.

    The following are the steps to monitor a call path initiated from a particular client:

    1. On the left-hand side panel of the Tuxedo component, select **Domain** from the drop-down list.
    2. On the right-hand side panel, the **Call Path** tab, select the **Enable** checkbox.
    3. Select the **Filter** checkbox with **Workstation Client**.
    4. Input a client name in the **Client Name** input box.
    5. Click on the **Add & Enable** button.

    The following step will help you to monitor the services of a particular server:

    The steps are similar to the call path monitoring policy, where you need to select options on the **Service** tab. In **Filter**, you can select a service from a list or input it manually.

5. Start to monitor Tuxedo.

    Log in to the TSAM console and start to monitor the Tuxedo system. The menu bar at the top contains the following Oracle TSAM monitoring console functionalities:

    ○ **Policy**: Define and manage system policies
    ○ **Tuxedo Metrics**: Query Tuxedo monitoring metrics
    ○ **Tuxedo Application Runtime Metrics**: Query Tuxedo Application Runtime monitoring metrics
    ○ **Management**: Define user management, data management, and global parameter settings
    ○ **Alert**: Define and query alerts
    ○ **Help**: The online help page

For details on the TSAM console user guide, you may refer to `http://docs.oracle.com/cd/E26665_01/tsam/docs11gr1/userguide/tsamconhelp.html`.

The logfiles

Though we can monitor Tuxedo in various ways (as previously discussed), logfiles are very important for an administrator for monitoring any Tuxedo application. Many times, the most important monitoring information will come from logfiles (for example, the TLOG, ULOG, and application logs). This type of information could be in the form of an error or warning message, a debug message, and an informational message, which is helpful in tracking and resolving problems in the system. Tuxedo provides the tracing capability through the `tmtrace()` function, and it can be used for ATMI servers and clients. All the messages are logged in the ULOG file as you set the `TMTRACE` environment variable (`TMTRACE=atmi:ulog`).

So, in this monitoring section, we have discussed four different ways a Tuxedo application can be monitored and changed: GUI, command-line interface, writing an MIB program, and looking at logfiles.

The important features of Tuxedo

In this section, we will discuss various important built-in features (security, data-dependent routing, encryption, and so on) that come with the Tuxedo system and how these features can be used to make your application more secure, effective, and responsive to address your business needs. These features are configurable, and there is no need to do any custom development, hence they are very cost-effective and easy to use.

Security

Security is one of biggest concerns for a Tuxedo administrator, and that is why Tuxedo provides mainly three levels of security features; in addition, Kerberos can be added for more.

- **First level**: This is provided by the operating system. This security imposes restrictions on the clients and the administrator.

- **Second level**: This is provided by Tuxedo. By default, any client program can join a Tuxedo application, but an application can be configured to ensure that all clients joining the application need to provide the password. There are many ways to restrict the client's access to the application.

- **Third level**: This is provided by an authentication service that checks for the combination of user identification, password, and client name, and it can connect to the Tuxedo application only if it passes this security.

There are mainly five types of incremental security provided by Tuxedo, which are as follows:

- **No authentication** (NONE): This level might be used in a development environment or in physically secured environments, as the clients do not need to be authenticated to join the application.

- **Application password** (APP-PW): This is a single password for the entire application; all the clients must provide this password to join the application.

- **End user authentication** (USER_AUTH): In this level, the client needs to provide a username and password; this is to customize the security for application-specific users to ensure that they can access the Tuxedo application.

- **Optional access control** (ACL): For all the previously mentioned levels, information needs to be provided by the client and the administrator so that access can be controlled to services, application queues, and events with access control lists. This level allows you to configure access only for those resources that need security; there is restricted access to a certain set of services while still allowing unprotected access to other services.

- **Mandatory access control** (MANDATORY_ACL): This is very similar to the ACL level; the only difference is that the resources without an ACL are considered restricted, that is, access is not granted to resources that do not have an ACL permission.

In this section, we have discussed all the different types of security features that you may like to consider to secure your Tuxedo application.

Data-dependent routing (DDR)

Data-dependent routing (or context-based routing) is used to enable a client to send requests for a service to have multiple/distributed copies of it; this is determined by the data in the requested message. Once an administrator has set up data-dependent routing for an application, the client requests can be routed automatically to servers based on the data in the requests. This DDR can be used in three different ways; we will discuss this in the following sections.

Horizontally partitioned

When a Tuxedo service is associated with a horizontally partitioned database (which means the database has been divided into segments), each segment is used to store a different category of information. As an example, there are different sections in a hospital (for example, ENT and cardiology). So, the same service can be called from different clients, but the request will be routed to the service-particular department server as the database was designed as horizontally partitioned.

Rule-based servers

A rule-based server is a server that determines whether service requests meet certain application-specific criteria before forwarding them to service routines. For example, in Banking, they have a Primer customer and a Normal customer, a distinction made for certain business reasons (high-value transactions), and the same service is served using two different servers. So, the features of the rule-based servers can be used when you want to handle requests that are almost the same, by taking slightly different actions for business reasons.

Distributed applications

In a distributed application, you may have a mix of local and remote clients that communicate with multiple servers that could be distributed in multiple geographic locations or machines across organizations over the network. A request is sent for a particular service; it is determined by the data identifying the server that can fulfill the request. The Tuxedo system selects a server to receive the request by matching the data to the routing criteria provided in the Bulletin Board. The ROUTING section of the UBBCONFIG file provides information for data-dependent routing of service requests using the FML, XML, and VIEWS types of buffer. You can also use DDR as a load-balancing mechanism by routing certain requests to a specific server.

Data encryption

Data encryption means converting data into a coded format that is unintelligible to all users except the user for which the data is intended. When encrypted data arrives at its destination, it is decrypted to convert back to its original format. Encrypting does not increase the data size, but it adds to processing time as the system needs to encrypt and decrypt the data. The data is compressed during encryption, so you may gain some time as less data is being sent across the network. When data is compressed, it helps to increase data security because the data is somewhat scrambled during compression. In the UBBCONFIG file, ENCRYPTION_REQUIRED can be specified in any of the four sections in the configuration hierarchy: the RESOURCES, MACHINES, GROUPS, or SERVICES section. Setting ENCRYPTION_REQUIRED to Y at a particular level means that encryption is required for all the running processes at that level or below it.

Data compression

This option shrinks an application buffer so that it can be transmitted more quickly over a network to different machine(s). You can set a maximum threshold value for the buffer size to ensure that it automatically compresses the buffer when it crosses the mark. The buffer gets compressed, but it gets decompressed as it reaches the destination. Data compression happens before the data is transported between machines; it improves network performance and enhances the security to a limit as it involves coding/decoding the data. In the UBBCONFIG file, the parameter CMPLIMT under the MACHINES section helps you set the threshold message size for messages bound to remote processes and local processes respectively, on which the automatic data compression will take place.

Load balancing

The load-balancing technique is used to distribute service requests evenly among servers that offer the same service(s) to ensure that some servers will not be overburdened while some are idle or infrequently used. The LDBAL parameter in the RESOURCES section of the UBBCONFIG file can be used to set the load balancing with Y. Also, the LOAD parameter under the SERVICES section refers to a number; this is very much a relative number you need to come up with according to the time required to execute that service. The statistics are generated based on this weightage for each server, and the Bulletin Board preserves this for each machine. Each Bulletin Board keeps a track of the increasing load associated with each of its servers; this is to ensure that when all the servers are busy, the Tuxedo system can select the one with the minimum load. You do need to do this if you have only a single service in one server, or servers in a single-queue (MSSQ) configuration.

In this section, we have discussed various important features of Tuxedo – security, routing, encryption, compression, and load balancing. Each of these features should be considered more carefully during the application, design, and deployment stage to make your application run more efficiently and to address your various business needs without any custom code.

Administering the Tuxedo queue (/Q)

Tuxedo provides a reliable queue based on the XA-compliant resource manager (TMS – Transaction Manager Server), which provides the framework to store messages in a reliable storage and forward it to different components. These could be services, clients, or components within different Tuxedo processes. The purpose of a queue is to perform time-independent communication. Any client or server can store onto (enqueue) and retrieve (dequeue) a message from the queue. Tuxedo provides the TMQUEUE server, which provides this enqueing and dequing service.

Tuxedo also provides a server called TMQFORWARD, which dequeues a message and forwards it to other services. Messages can be retrieved in any of several ordering schemes, including Last In, First Out (LIFO), First In, First Out (FIFO), priority order, and time-based order. More than one client or server can access the same queue. In *Chapter 3, Development of Tuxedo – Various APIs*, I have discussed the Tuxedo queue in more detail; I am avoiding repetition, so please refer to the *Queues (Tuxedo /Q)* section of that chapter.

There are three primary tasks for a Tuxedo administrator to carry out. They are configuring, maintaining, and monitoring the Tuxedo queue.

Configuration of resources for /Q

There are three servers (TMS, TMQUEUE, and TMQFORWARD) provided by the Tuxedo system that need to be configured in the SERVER section of the UBBCONFIG file.

Also, there must be a server group defined for each queue space as per the application usage or design. The TMSNAME and OPENINFO parameters need to be set accordingly; please see the following example in the UBBCONFIG file:

```
*GROUPS
TMQUEUE-G1   GRPNO=1 TMSNAME=TMS_QM
             OPENINFO="TUXEDO/QM:/dev/deviceONE:QueueSpace1"

*SERVERS
TMQUEUE    SRVGRP="TMQUEUE-G1" SRVID=1550 RESTART=Y GRACE=0 \
           CLOPT="-s CUSTOMER:TMQUEUE"
```

In this example, the -s flag of the CLOPT parameter is used to name the queue space served by a given instance of the server.

 We mentioned that the environment variable for the queue (/Q) is QMCONFIG, which needs to be set in the environment.

Creation of queue space and queues

To use a queue, we need to create the queue devices, queue space, and queues, in that order; qmadmin is the tool provided by the Tuxedo system to do this for us.

%UnixPromt%> qmadmin

> crdl /home/applicationQ/CustomerQdev 0 500

At this point, your device is created with a size of 500 physical pages beginning/ offset at block 0; you need to create the queue space next.

```
> qspacecreate
Queue space name: QueueSpace1
IPC Key for queue space: 12345
Size of queue space in disk pages: 300
Number of queues in queue space: 3
Number of concurrent transactions in queue space: 4
Number of concurrent processes in queue space: 4
Number of messages in queue space: 20
Error queue name: ErrorQ
Initialize extents (y, n [default=n]): y
Blocking factor [default=16]: 16
```

You have created the queue space and now you need to create a queue using the same qmadmin command.

```
> qcreate
Queue name: Customer
Queue order (priority, time, fifo, lifo): fifo
Out-of-ordering enqueuing (top, msgid, [default=none]): none
Retries [default=0]: 2
Retry delay in seconds [default=0]: 30
High limit for queue capacity warning (b for bytes used, B for blocks
used,
% for percent used, m for messages [default=100%]): 80%
Reset (low) limit for queue capacity warning [default=0%]: 0%
Queue capacity command:
No default queue capacity command
Queue  Customer created
```

You have created the Customer queue; use the same steps to create ErrorQ before you exit out of this tool.

Note that if you need more space for the queue space, you can do that by using the qaddext command.

Monitoring /Q

Using qmadmin as the command-line tool or using the Tuxedo console, you can configure, monitor, and change queues in a Tuxedo application. It has a rich set of options (30+) to choose from.

In this section, we discussed Tuxedo /Q, which is one of the most important components of Tuxedo for reliable messaging. Tuxedo itself uses /Q for its internal process communication. The Tuxedo administrator is responsible for defining servers and creating queue spaces and queues using qmadmin, as described, and must define at least one queue server group with TMS_QM as the transaction manager server for the group. For more information, please refer to the *Queues (Tuxedo /Q)* section of the next chapter.

The Tuxedo domain

The Tuxedo domain can be used for large-federated or distributed-application architecture across cities, countries, or different parts of the world. The Tuxedo domain facilitates interoperate or extend the scope of various applications to include access to other Tuxedo and non-Tuxedo-based applications. The Tuxedo domain provides transparency between applications to ensure that any client can get services from another domain (remote service) by maintaining the security norms. The Tuxedo administrator can define/design different domains based on the geographical location of the data center or to enforce inter-organizational boundaries. The Tuxedo domains are autonomous, which means they are administered independently of each other. Domains are defined by the administrator; he/she defines how the services in one domain are made available to another. There are basically three components for the Tuxedo domain architecture: DoMain Administrative server (DMADM), GateWay Administrative server (GWADM), and Domain Gateway server (GWTDOMAIN), which I have briefly discussed later.

Please refer to the following diagram for more clarity:

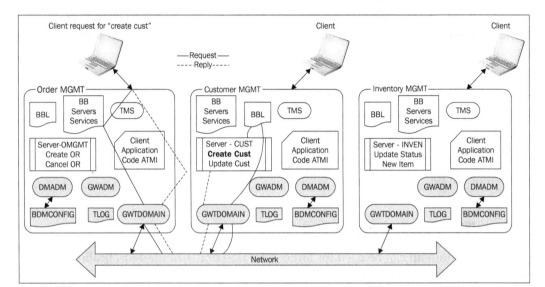

The domain configuration file

The domain configuration file is a text file very similar to the UBBCONFIG file, and it is called the DMCONFIG file. The dmloadcf command converts this text file to a binary file called BDMCONFIG. You need to create a separate DMCONFIG file for each Oracle Tuxedo domain participating in the configuration. Please make sure that the DMCONFIG environment variable is set on each domain.

The domain gateway server

This Tuxedo-provided server communicates with other domains. It also supports multiple networks, multiple domains, transaction management, multiple communication modules (request/reply, queue-based, and conversational), and Tuxedo buffer types.

The domain administrative server

Tuxedo's Domain Administrative server, DMADM, is used to administer a domain configuration. A domain gateway group has a GWADM server, which is a gateway administrative server, one GWTDOMAIN, which is a domain gateway server, and a TLOG, which is optional. Please refer to the previous diagram. The GWADM server allows runtime administration of the domain gateway. A DMADM server helps with the administration of the Tuxedo domain configuration file (BDMCONFIG).

Administrative tools for the domain

Like all other Tuxedo components, an administrator has to monitor and maintain the Tuxedo domain. There are three basic administrative commands provided by the Tuxedo system, and they are as follows:

- dmloadcf() – This reads and checks the syntax of the DMCONFIG file and converts it to a binary BDMCONFIG configuration file.

- dmunloadcf() – This translates the BDMCONFIG configuration file to text format.

- dmadmin() – This is the runtime tool to enable administrators to configure, monitor, and tune domain gateway groups dynamically, and to update the domain configuration files. The dmadmin command with the -c option enters into the configuration mode to update or add new configuration information to the BDMCONFIG file of the domain's configuration file. It requires the use of the DMADM server for the administration of the BDMCONFIG file, and the GWADM server for the reconfiguration of active domain gateway groups. So, you need to run one DMADM server and one GWADM server for each domain gateway group in a domain.

Creating a domain transaction log

You need to create a domain transaction log before you start a domain gateway group. This needs to be created for the local domain; the machine on which DMADM is running.

You need to use the dmadmin tools to create it.

```
>dmadmin crdmlog crdlog -d local_domain_name
```

This command uses the parameters specified in the DMCONFIG file. This command fails if the local domain name is active on the current machine or if a log already exists.

The dmadmin command has a huge set of options, so please refer to following URL for more details:

```
http://docs.oracle.com/cd/E26665_01/tuxedo/docs11gr1/rfcm/rfcmd.
html#wp998708
```

A brief example of how to configure and run a Tuxedo domain

1. Edit your UBBCONFIG file to add the domain administrative servers and the TDomain gateway server.

```
*GROUPS
DMADM-GROUP    LMID=Alpha    GRPNO=1
GWT-GROUP    LMID=Beta    GRPNO=2

*SERVERS
DMADM      SRVGRP=DMADM-GROUP
SRVID=2001
REPLYQ=N
RESTART=Y
GRACE=0
GWADM    SRVGRP=GWT-GROUP
SRVID=2002
REPLYQ=N
RESTART=Y
GRACE=0
GWTDOMAIN    SRVGRP=GWT-GROUP
SRVID=3003
RQADDR="GWT-GROUP"
REPLYQ=N
RESTART=Y
GRACE=0
```

2. Create TUXCONFIG by running tmloadcf() on this new UBBCONFIG file.

3. Now you need to edit the DMCONFIG file, as follows:

```
*DM_LOCAL
LOCAL-ONE       GWGRP=GWT-GROUP
                  TYPE=TDOMAIN
                  ACCESSPOINTID="USA. 01"
                  BLOCKTIME=30
                  CONNECTION_POLICY=ON_STARTUP
                  MAXRETRY=5
                  RETRY_INTERVAL=100
*DM_REMOTE
REMOTE-ONE     TYPE=TDOMAIN   ACCESSPOINTID="USA.02"
REMOTE-TWO     TYPE=TDOMAIN   ACCESSPOINTID="USA.03"
*DM_EXPORT
LTOLOWER     LACCESSPOINT=LOCAL-ONE
                    CONV=N
                    RNAME="TOLOWER"
```

```
*DM_IMPORT
RTOUPPER        AUTOTRAN=N
                RACCESSPOINT=REMOTE-ONE
                LACCESSPOINT=LOCAL-ONE
                CONV=N
                RNAME="TOUPPER"
*DM_TDOMAIN
LOCAL-ONE       NWADDR="//203.0.0.01:4444"
REMOTE-ONE      NWADDR="//305.0.0.99:4455"
REMOTE-TWO      NWADDR="//309.0.0.99:4466"
```

The DMCONFIG file should be in the same machine where the DMADM server is running.

4. You should run dmloadcf on this DMCONFIG file to create the BDMCONFIG binary file to the location referenced by the BDMCONFIG environment variable.

5. Start the Oracle Tuxedo application servers by running tmboot. You may check if all the domain-related servers are up and running.

In this section, we discussed the Tuxedo domain, which is mainly used when a company grows. A company's IT department may need to organize and manage their business information in a different manner, which consists of various applications with different functionality or located in multiple locations. This Tuxedo domain's feature helps in segregating infrastructure for simplifying the solution while maintaining seamless interoperability among the business applications.

For more detailed information on Tuxedo domain configuration, please refer to the Oracle website at http://docs.oracle.com/cd/E26665_01/tuxedo/docs11gr1/add/addomc.html.

Tuning the application

Planning the architecture of a Tuxedo system is a very important and critical task, as there are a number of components that have various parameters that can impact performance, scalability, reliability, and security. There are basically two major areas we need to look at: **modularity** (which makes applications more manageable), and **agile and resource management** (which means sharing common resources to reduce maintenance, that is, time and cost). As an administrator, you need to keep these two in mind, and you don't need to predefine the application configuration all at once. The initial/default values for parameters in UBBCONFIG usually provide acceptable/standard performance in most cases. If the performance, measured by response time, is not as high as required, the administrator should monitor the system to determine the bottleneck and change parameters as necessary. I am sharing some practical experiences with you, which are very common, but critical for a Tuxedo system.

You may need to look at the following areas:

- The service is running slow:
  - ○ It could be SQL, which is running slow because of join or indexing.
  - ○ You could be making a large number of database accesses or retrieving a large amount of data.
  - ○ The queue may fill up with a number of waiting service requests, increasing the number of instances of the servers providing the services.
  - ○ Many times, one server can have multiple services in it, and one or more of them can be a long-running service. This long-running service(s) can hold the process for a longer time, and no other services can be used during that time, making sure that the mixing of services in a server is properly done.

- Queues are very important in the system; you need to monitor queues very closely, as they may get full and the whole system can become slow or even hang.

- The network is another area that we usually overlook, but it can also affect the Tuxedo application. You may use `tmadmin` to monitor the basic network usage, but having a good tool for network management will be very helpful.

- Hardware is another area that can cause slowdowns. If the platform is heavily loaded, it may be necessary to tune the server (Unix kernel parameters – shared memory, message queues, and semaphores); if you think you have done enough and it is still slow/loaded, add more hardware to take up the load.

- Check if a service uses too many CPU cycles. You may need to involve the development team to redesign the service.

- The database needs to be tuned many times as it tends to be overlooked.

- It is not recommended to have a service calling another service in the same server, as it may cause a bottleneck.

- Do not use the Multiple Server Single Queue (MSSQ) without looking at its usage and throughput.

- There could be some problem when servers restart themselves multiple times, and you may not notice it as you see some of them are up at any given time. Restarting a server loads the system a great deal, and that can slow down the application, so please look at the ULOG and check for any kind of behavior like this.

- Many times we can use multiple nodes (MP mode), but do not use the `Migrate` feature in the `RESOURCE` section.

Summary

In this chapter, we discussed various components of a Tuxedo application from the administrative perspective. I explained the configuration file and its structure and the relevance of its parameters. I have listed all the Tuxedo commands and how to monitor a Tuxedo application using these commands and TSAM's web-based GUI interface. I have also explained the Tuxedo queue and the reliable-messaging mechanism and how to create and administer it. The Tuxedo domain is another important component that can be used for real-time distributed applications spread across geographical and organizational boundaries. We discussed various built-in features of Tuxedo (for example, load balancing and data-dependent routing) that make Tuxedo more robust, scalable, and easy to use. Each of these sections itself is a vast topic, and a book can be written on each of them. The intention of this book is to give you a quick overview of each of these important components of Tuxedo. In the end, we discussed some of the practical tuning guidelines you should consider for better throughput, utilization, and stability of a Tuxedo system.

3
Development of
Tuxedo – Various APIs

The Tuxedo application interface is called **Application-to-Transaction Monitor Interface (ATMI)**. In this chapter, we will discuss how to use these interfaces to build your applications—combinations of the client and server modules, Tuxedo buffer types, communication paradigms, and transactions (XA). These ATMIs are very rich and could be overwhelming to start with, so my intention is to give you a quick overview of each of their categories and some brief characteristics so that you are able to design and build a standard Tuxedo application quickly. The two primary languages used for writing a Tuxedo application are C and COBOL; C++ is also used for the object-oriented version of Tuxedo, which is CORBA-based (this is not discussed in this book).

Introduction to the Application Programing Interface

The core interfaces for Tuxedo are defined in C and COBOL, but there are also some third-party languages available for developing a Tuxedo application. As a developer, you will be able to choose the platform for a Tuxedo client/server based on the ease of development, debugging tools, performance/overhead, and expertise.

Here I have listed most of the Tuxedo ATMI interfaces for C and COBOL for quick reference. We will discuss them in more detail in the following sections of this chapter.

ATMI type	C API	COBOL API	Comments
Client	tpinit()	TPINITIALIZE	Allows a client program to join an application
	tpterm()	TPTERM	Allows a client to leave the application
	tpchkauth()	TPCHKAUTH	Checks if authentication is needed
Communication (request/ response)	tpcall()	TPCALL	Synchronous call to a service
	tpacall()	TPACALL	Asynchronous call to a service
	tpgetreply()	TPGETREPLY	Gets a reply back for an asynchronous call
	tpcancel()	TPCANCLE	Cancels an asynchronous call to a service
Communication (conversational)	tpconnect()	TPCONNECT	Used to start a conversational connection with a service
	tpdiscon()	TPDISCON	Disconnects from a conversational connection
	tpsend()	TPSEND	Sends a message during a conversation
	tprecv()	TPRECV	Receives a message during a conversation

ATMI type	C API	COBOL API	Comments
Communication (event-based)	tpnotify()	TPNOTIFY	Notifies the client with an unsolicited message
	tpbroadcast()	TPBROADCAST	To send an unsolicited message to all clients
	tpsetunsol()	TPSETUNSOL	Set a callback for an unsolicited message
	tpchkunsol()	TPCHKUNSOL	To check if there is any unsolicited message
	tppost()	TPPOST	To post an event message
	tpsubscribe()	TPSUBSCRIBE	To subscribe for an event
	tpunsubscribe()	TPUNSUBSCRIBE	Unsubscribes an event
	-	TPGETUNSOL	Catches an unsolicited message
Message precedence	tpgprio()	TPGPRIO	Gets the last request's priority
	tpsprio()	TPSPRIO	To set the next request's priority
Memory management	tpalloc()	-	Creates a message-allocate memory
	tprealloc()	-	Reallocates (resizing) a message
	tpfree()	-	Free message
	tptypes()	-	Gets a message type
Server/service	tpsvrinit()	TPSVRINIT	To initialize a server
	tpsvrdone()	TPSVRDONE	To terminate a server
	tpreturn()	TPRETURN	End of service
	tpforward()	TPFORWARD	Forwards a request to another service
	-	TPSVCSTART	Gets service information; only for the COBOL interface

ATMI type	C API	COBOL API	Comments
Transaction management (XA)	tpbegin()	TPBEGIN	To start an XA/ transaction
	tpcommit()	TPCOMMIT	Commits a transaction
	tpabort()	TPABORT	Aborts or rolls back a transaction
	tpgetlev()	TPGETLEV	To check the mode of a transaction
	tpsuspend()	TPSUSPEND	To suspend a transaction
	tpresume()	TPRESUME	To resume a suspended transaction
	tmscmt()	TPSCMT	Controls a commit return
Resources management	tpopen()	TPOPEN	Opens a resource manager (RM) to which a caller is linked
	tpclose()	TPCLOSE	To close a resource manager (RM)
Queuing	tpenqueue()	TPENQUEUE	To push a message in a queue
	tpdequeue()	TPDEQUEUE	To pick up a message from a queue
Dynamic service advertisement	tpadvertise()	TPADVERTISE	Advertises a service dynamically
	tpunadvertise()	TPUNADVERTISE	Dynamically unadvertises a service name

ATMI type	C API	COBOL API	Comments
Buffer-related	tpconvert()	-	Transforms the structures to/from a string
	tpconvmb()	-	Transforms the encoded characters in an input buffer to a named target
	tpexport()	-	Transforms a typed buffer into an exportable, machine-independent string, which embraces encryption seals and digital signatures
Security and administration	tpcryptpw()	-	Administrative request to encrypt an application's password
	tpgetadmkey()	-	To get an administrative authentication key
	tuxgetenv()	-	Returns a value for environment variables set for Tuxedo
	tuxputenv()	-	To dynamically add/change a value to the environment variable
	tpadmcall()	-	Administers may use this to retrieve and update the attributes of a service
System error-handling	tpstrerror()	-	To capture an error message for a Tuxedo ATMI
	tpstrerrordetail()	-	To capture the detailed error message for a Tuxedo ATMI
	userlog()	USERLOG	To write a message (error or warning) from any Tuxedo application to the system's central log

The C language interface for the previously mentioned interfaces makes use of the full range of C language features—pointer, allocation of buffer, C data structure, and so on. The COBOL interfaces provide similar semantics and functionality as that of the C interfaces. The COBOL programmer will find it comfortable to use these semantics. In our book, we will only be describing all the ATMI interfaces for the C language.

Developing a Tuxedo client

A client is an application program that initiates requests in the Tuxedo application. This can be built in different platforms (for example, in both terminal and graphical interfaces). A client has to join the application before it can make any request to a server/service and must leave the application before exiting.

There are basically two types of clients:

- **Native client**: This runs on the same platform as the Tuxedo domain, meaning it is attached locally
- **Workstation (WS) client**: This runs on a different machine and joins over the network to a Tuxedo application running on a different machine

The design, coding, and operation of these two types of clients are the same—the ATMI for both are identical. There are some differences in the way these clients are compiled using the `buildclient` command, which will be described later.

Your client application uses `tpinit()` to attach to a Tuxedo application and `tpterm()` to detach from it. When a client joins an application, a username and client name can be passed to the `tpinit()` structure; these are string values of up to 30 characters. The user and client name are used to identify a client program in several important ways:

- **Security**: This is used when the application security is configured on a per-user-password basis; the client program must provide a password that matches the password for the user/client
- **Administration**: The administrator can see who is connected to the application
- **Communication**: Either one or all the clients can be communicated to via their individual name using `tpbrodcast()`/`tpnotify()`

There are four paradigms for client/server communication:

- **Request/response**: A client program sends a request to a server/service and waits for the server/services' response before it executes any other operation that is synchronous in nature. A client uses the `tpcall()` function to invoke this kind of communication in Tuxedo. There is an asynchronous way of doing such communication where the client can send the request and get the reply later, as needed. This is a stateless communication, and `tpacall()` and `tpgetreply()` are used for this type of communication.

- **Conversational**: This is similar to request/reply, but in a more conversational mode, where request and reply come back and forth from the client and servers. This is a stateful communication, and Tuxedo provides the `tpconnect()`, `tpsend()`, `tprecv()`, and `tpdiscon()` ATMI functions.

- **Queuing**: Many times, a client program may need to communicate in online mode (as in the previous two paradigms); we can call it a time-independent communication, where the client puts the message(s) in a reliable queue and not in an online mode with those that pick up the message from the queue. There are two functions in ATMI, namely `tpenqueue()` and `tpdequeue()`.

- **Publish and subscribe (Pub-sub)**: This communication between the client and servers is based on an event. There are three functions associated with it, namely `tpsetunsol()`, `tpnotify()`, and `tpbroadcast()`. A client has to register to an application using `tpsetunsol()`; and then, if anybody (client or server) generates an unsolicited message using one of `tpnotify()` or `tpbroadcast()`, it gets that notification accordingly.

Sample client code structure

The basic client code structure using Tuxedo ATMI is shown in the following code snippet:

```
# Include Tuxedo and c lib using #include
main()
{
Use tpalloc() to allocate TPINIT buffer
You may require to pass user/cltname/password in the TPINIT buffer as
per you security set up.
tpinit() to join the Tuxedo application
Send service request using tpcall()/ tpacall()
Receive reply - you need to use tpgetreply() for using tpacall()
Process the reply as per your requirements
leave application using tpterm()
}
```

Once you write the client code, you need to compile it using the `buildclient` command provided by Tuxedo. The same code can be used for the native or workstation client; please check the following section for more details.

Compiling the native or workstation client

Tuxedo provides the `buildclient` command to compile a Tuxedo client.

```
buildclient [-C] [ -v ] [ {-r rmname | -w } ] [ -o name] [ -f 1st-file
name ] [ -l last-file name]
```

- -v – Verbose mode; to display the compilation message
- -w – To build the workstation client in such a way that it uses WS libraries
- -r – This specifies the resource manager (RM) related/linked with this client
- -o – The outputted executable filename
- -f – The source code file(s) to be included first in the compilation and link-edit phases of `buildclient`
- -l – The file(s) to be included last in the compilation and link-edit phases of `buildclient`
- -C – This is to specify COBOL compilation

An example of compiling a native client call, `my_client`, is as follows:

```
> buildclient -o my_client  -f  my_client.c
```

An example of compiling a WS client call, `my_client`, is as follows:

```
> buildclient  -w  -o  my_client  -f  my_client.c
```

Tuxedo client ATMI functions

The following is a list of Tuxedo client ATMI commands along with their syntax:

- tpinit – int tpinit(TPINIT *tpinfo)
- tpcall – int tpcall(char *service, char *indata, long ilen, char **outdata, long *olen, long flags)
- tpacall – int tpacall(char *service, char *indata, long length, long flags)
- tpgetreply – int tpgetrply(int *cd, char **indata, long *length, long flags)

- tpenqueue – int tpenqueue(char *q-space, char *q-name, TPQCTL *ctl, char *indata, long length, long flags)

- tpdqueue – int tpdequeue(char *q-space, char *q-name, TPQCTL *ctl, char **indata, long *length, long flags)

- tpnotify – int tpnotify(CLIENTID *client-id, char *indata, long length, long flags)

- tpbroadcast – int tpbroadcast(char *lmid-clt, char *usr-name, char *clt-name, char *indata, long length, long flags)

- tpsetunsol – void (*tpsetunsol (void (_TMDLLENTRY *)(*displ) (char *indata, long length, long flags))) (char *indata, long length, long flags)

- tpconnect – int tpconnect(char *service, char *indata, long length, long flags)

- tpsend – int tpsend(int c-descriptor, char *indata, long length, long flags, long *r-event)

- tprecv – int tprecv(int c-descriptor, char **indata, long *length, long flags, long *r-event)

- tpdiscon – int tpdiscon(int c-descriptor)

- tpforward – tpforward(char *service, char *indata, long length, long flags)

- tpalloc – char * tpalloc(char *Btype, char *sub-type, long sizeofbuf)

- tpchkauth – int tpchkauth(void)

- tpterm – int tpterm(void)

For more information on each of these interfaces, please refer to the following URL:

http://docs.oracle.com/cd/E26665_01/tuxedo/docs11gr1/rf3c/rf3c.html#wp1022852

Developing a Tuxedo server

We discussed the Tuxedo client in the previous section and now we'll discuss how to develop a Tuxedo server for a client's request or for other servers that call a server to get some work done and finally return it to the client. The Tuxedo server provides services (business functions) to the client or other servers. It starts the process as it gets the request and replies back to its caller. A service must be made known (advertised) in such a way that another client or server can call it.

The servers are started when a Tuxedo application is booted (`tmboot`), and they do the following two things:

- `tpsvrinit()`, which is a callback function, is called after the server is connected to an application, but before processing any application request. If an XA resource manager is being used with the server, `tpopen()` connects to the resource manager using OPENINFO from the UBBCONFIG file.

- The server registers itself with a Bulletin Board as available for processing any request and waits for a new request to come in.

Sample server code structure

There are basically three sections of a server: `tpsvrinit()` to initialize the server; `MyService()` to specify the service in the business logic; and lastly `tpsvrdone()` when you need to close any connections to the database or resources manager. The default function can be used if there is no termination logic.

```
/* Need to "#include" c and Tuxedo library and header files  */
tpsvrinit (int argc, char *argv[])
{
 /* do all initialization working for server e.g. connecting to
database etc. */
      return(0);
 }

MyService(TPSVCINFO *rqst)
 {

  /* Write My Service logic here to do specific job */
     tpreturn (TPSUCCESS, 0, rqst->data, 0L, 0);
 }
tpsvrdone (void)
{
/* close any connection to database before server get shutdown */

 }
```

Advertising a service

There are four different ways we can advertise a service:

- **Compile time**: This is the normal way, where we mention the service name when compiling the server using the `buildserver` command with the `-s` option in it. By default, a service name is assumed to map to a service's entry-point name with an identical name. This approach is static and determined at build time.

- **Configuration time**: The command-line options can be used to specify the service names to be advertised.

- **Administratively**: This administrative GUI- or API-based approach can be used to advertise or unadvertise a service. This is basically a dynamic approach.

- **Runtime using ATMI**: A service can be dynamically advertised using `tpadvertise()`. This is usually done during the server-initialization routine. It is also possible to advertise a service dynamically from another service.

Tuxedo server ATMI functions

The following is a list of Tuxedo server ATMI commands along with their syntax:

- `tpsvrinit` – `int tpsvrinit (int argc, char **argv)`

- `tpsvrdone` – `tpsvrdone()`

- `tpreturn` – `tpreturn(int r-val, int r-code, char *indata, long length, long flags)`

- `tpforward` – `tpforward(char *servicename, char *indata, long length, long flags)`

- `tpadvertise` – `int tpadvertise(char *servicename, void *function)`

- `tpunadvertise` – `tpunadvertise(char * servicename)`

For more detailed information on each of these interfaces, please refer to the following URL:

`http://docs.oracle.com/cd/E26665_01/tuxedo/docs11gr1/rf3c/rf3c.html#wp1022852`

How to compile a server

Tuxedo provides the `buildserver` command to construct a Tuxedo server module.

```
buildserver [-C] [-M] [-s services[:func[()]]] [-v] [-o out-file] [-f
1st-file] [-l last-file] [{-r|-g} RM-name] [{-r|-g} rmid:RM-name] [-E
env-label] [-t]
```

The following are the attributes of the previous command:

- `-C` – This attribute stipulates the COBOL compilation

- `-M` – This specifies the server to be associated with multiple XA-compliant resource managers, and this his option is mandatory

- -s – This specifies the name(s) of the service(s) that can be advertised when the server boots

- -v – This option puts the compilation on verbose mode; all messages during compilation can be seen

- -o – This option specifies the filename of the executable

- -f – The filename(s) that needs to be included for linking before the Tuxedo ATMI libraries

- -l – The filename(s) that needs to be included for linking after the Tuxedo ATMI libraries

- -r – The resource manager (RM) related to the server or that needs to be attached to the server

In this section, we have discussed the structure of the server along with the various essentials to build a server module.

Tuxedo buffer types

The Tuxedo-based application is a message-driven application, and these messages can use different types of buffers. In this section, we will be focusing on all five types of buffers. Tuxedo supports STRING, VIEW, CARRAY, FML, and XML. All these buffer types can be transmitted over a network within heterogeneous systems. The Tuxedo system handles translations and data conversions between machines with different operating systems.

The STRING buffer

This is the most simple type of buffer with a string of characters. It has a null-terminated string. This buffer cannot be used for data-dependent routing. tpalloc() can be used to allocate the STRING buffer with the desired length. The following code snippet helps you with allocating the STRING buffer type:

```
char *stringPtr;
 . . .
stringPtr = tpalloc("STRING", NULL, 0);
```

The CARRAY buffer

This is another simple form of buffer that is basically used to transmit binary data. The Tuxedo system does not interpret the character of the CARRAY buffer type in any other way. The CARRAY buffer is not self-describing like other buffer types. This buffer cannot be used for data-dependent routing. You can use tpalloc() with the type set to CARRAY with the desired length. The following code snippet helps you with how to allocate the CARRAY type:

```
char *carrayPtr;
long carraysize;
. . .
carraysize = 1024;
carrayPtr = tpalloc ("CARRAY", NULL, carraysize);
```

The VIEW buffer

This type of buffer is very similar to the standard C language structure or a COBOL record that has an associated definition for the fields with their types. This does not support a structure inside the structure or arrays of structures or pointers. VIEW supports integral types (integer, char, and decimal) and can be converted to FML and vice versa. There are two variations of VIEW: normal VIEW, which uses C language's short integer to store a field; and VIEW32, which uses a long integer to do the same.

You need to take the following steps to use VIEW/VIEW32:

1. Define the VIEW structure in a file.
2. You need to compile using viewc or viewc32 with the -n option to create a view file and a header file, which needs to be included in your program for both the client and the server.
3. Then set the environment variable VIEWFILES/VIEWFILES32 with your view file and VIEWDIR/VIEWDIR32 pointing to the directory of the view file.

The following is a sample of a VIEW file:

```
VIEW SampleView
#TYPE       CNAME       FBNAME        COUNT       FLAG      SIZE      NULL
String      Str1        Str1          4           -         10        -
Char        Char1       Char1         1           -         -         -
Long        Long1       long1         1           -         -         -
END
```

The following are the attributes of a VIEW file:

- TYPE – This specifies the data type (Short, Long, Char, and so on)
- CNAME – This is the variable name in the structure
- FBNAME –This is the FML name that is needed to exchange the VIEW and FML types and vice versa
- COUNT – This specifies the fields with multiple occurrences
- FLAG – This is to control mapping types for VIEW with other buffer types
- SIZE –This specifies the size of the field
- NULL – This is the application-defined null value for the field

The following code snippet helps you with allocating the VIEW type:

```
struct SampleView * SampleViewPtr;  /* pointer to SampleView
structure */
: : :
SampleViewPtr = (struct SampleView *) tpalloc("VIEW", " SampleView",
sizeof(struct SampleView));
```

The FML buffer

FML stands for **Field Manipulation Language**. This is very much like a tag/value pair. It provides a rich set of C functions to manipulate the buffer, where you can create, modify, delete, and access a field, and much more. There are two types of FML: FML16 and FML32.

You need to perform the following steps to use FML16/FML32:

1. Create the FML field table files.
2. Use the mkfldhdr or mkfldhdr32 command to create a header file for both the client and server programs.

   ```
   >mkfldhdr [-d path for header files are written ] [FML_field_
   table….]
   ```

   It will create a header file with the .h extension.

3. Set the environment variable FIELDTBLS/FIELDTBLS32 with the name of the header files separated by a comma and FLDTBLDIR/FLDTBLDIR32 with directories separated by a colon for the FML16/FML32 files.

The following is a sample of an FML file:

```
SampleFML
* Base 200
```

#NAME	NUMBER	TYPE	FLAGs	Comments
Name	200	String	-	Customer name
Age	220	long	-	Customer age

The following are the attributes of an FML file:

- *Base value – This specifies a baseline for offsetting succeeding field numbers
- NAME –This specifies the identifier for the field
- NUMBER – This specifies the relative value of the field in numbers
- TYPE –This specifies the type of the field
- FLAGs – This is not used at present
- Comments – This is just for documentation purposes

The following code snippet helps you with allocating memory for the FML buffer:

```
FBFR *fmlPrt;      /* c-pointer to an FML type buffer */
 ::
fmlPtr = (FBFR *) tpalloc("FML", NULL, Fneeded(f, v))
```

FML has a very rich set of functions as a manipulation language—they number around 100. So, I do not intend to explain them in this section, but I have listed them so that you know what they are.

CFadd, CFadd32(), CFchg, CFchg32(), CFfind, CFfind32(), CFfindocc, CFfindocc32(), CFget, CFget32(), CFgetalloc, CFgetalloc32(), F_error, F_error32(), Fadd, Fadd32(), Fadds, Fadds32(), Falloc, Falloc32(1), Fboolco, Fboolco32, Fvboolco, Fvboolco32(), Fboolev, Fboolev32, Fvboolev, Fvboolev32(), Fboolpr, Fboolpr32, Fvboolpr, Fvboolpr32(), Fchg, Fchg32(1), Fchgs, Fchgs32(), Fchksum, Fchksum32(), Fcmp, Fcmp32(), Fconcat, Fconcat32(), Fcpy, Fcpy32(), Fdel, Fdel32(), Fdelall, Fdelall32(), Fdelete, Fdelete32(), Fextread, Fextread32(), Ffind, Ffind32(), Ffindlast, Ffindlast32(), Ffindocc, Ffindocc32(), Ffinds, Ffinds32(), Ffloatev, Ffloatev32, Fvfloatev, Fvfloatev32(), Ffprint, Ffprint32(), Ffree, Ffree32(), Fget, Fget32(), Fgetalloc, Fgetalloc32(), Fgetlast, Fgetlast32(), Fgets, Fgets32(), Fgetsa, Fgetsa32(), Fidxused, Fidxused32(), Fielded, Fielded32(), Findex, Findex32(), Finit, Finit32(), Fjoin, Fjoin32(), Fldid, Fldid32(), Fldno, Fldno32(), Fldtype, Fldtype32(), Fidnm_unload, and Fidnm_unload32().

Refer to the following URL for more information:

http://docs.oracle.com/cd/E26665_01/tuxedo/docs11gr1/fml/fml05.html#wp1056761

The XML buffer

The XML buffer type can be used by a Tuxedo application for messaging. The Tuxedo application can use the simple XML buffers. All the logic to manipulate XML documents (for example, parsing) exists in the application. You can use `tpalloc()` to create the buffer with a maximum size of 4 GB. Data-dependent routing can be used with XML.

An XML document has the following:

- The characters in an order that encodes the text of a document
- An explanation of the logical structure of the document and information about that structure
- An XML parser in the Tuxedo systems, which works as follows:
  - Auto-detection of encoded characters
  - Character code conversion
  - Detection of element content and attribute values
  - Data type conversion

XML has been accepted as a standard buffer type and is widely used. Tuxedo has adopted it and many new developments have been done using XML rather than using any other buffer types. The old traditional Tuxedo FML buffer can be converted to and from XML. There are more steps to follow, and third-party tools can also be helpful. For more information on the XML buffer type, please refer to the following URL:

```
http://docs.oracle.com/cd/E26665_01/tuxedo/docs11gr1/pgc/pgbuf.
html#wp1274232
```

So, in this section, we have discussed all the five types of buffers that Tuxedo supports, and you will be able to pick the best fit for your application design.

Client/server communication paradigms

In this section, we will discuss client/server communication paradigms. There are four different ways these communications can take place, namely request/reply, conversational, communication by using a queue, and event-based. There is a single namespace for all the service names, so from an administrative point of view, a service name can be defined as either request/response or conversational. A request/reply service can be called using `tpcall()`, `tpacall()`, or `tpforward()`; `tpconnect()` can only be used to call a conversational service.

Request/reply

This works in the following ways:

1. First it receives one request at a time and handles one request at a time.

2. Then it returns (using `tpreturn()`) or forwards (using `tpforward()`) the result.

 Using `tpforward()` to invoke a service in the same server works, but it is not considered a best practice as it defeats the purpose of using `tpforward()` to free up the server to process more requests.

Conversational

A service can become conversational by configuring and cannot be called using any other ATMI interface except `tpconnect()`. The following are the characteristics of conversational communication:

- May send and receive one or multiple messages with the caller

- May initiate with other conversational services

- Should not be using `tpforward()`

- Must end the conversation with the caller with `tpreturn()`

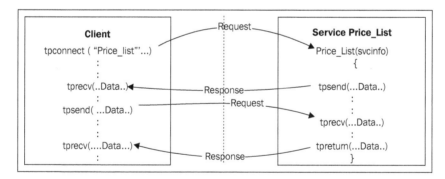

Queues (Tuxedo /Q)

Tuxedo's reliable queue is another communication paradigm that has been used internally within Tuxedo's internal process communication, and it can be used for client/server communication as well. We have discussed the Tuxedo queue in the two previous chapters from an administrative point of view, and in this section we will be discussing how a developer can use the Tuxedo queue APIs to initiate more reliable communication within the application's components.

The application queue is ideal to use when an application needs to communicate in an asynchronous manner or both parties are not online at the same time. This allows an application to put a message into the disk-based (or file-based) queue so that a message can be dequeued in a logical order. Both the enqueuing and dequeuing process can be done by a client or server and both these processes are transactional (XA-compliant), which ensures no message loss and therefore improved reliability. TMS_QM is the transaction resource manager, which works with all the queue servers (TMQUEUE and TMQFORWARD) provided by Tuxedo.

The TMQUEUE server provides enqueuing and dequeuing services. The enqueuing process calls tx_begin() to start a transaction and then enqueues the message and ends the transaction with tx_commit(). The message is ready to be dequeued once enqueuing is done. Similarly, to dequeue a message, this dequeue process starts the transaction, dequeues the message, and delivers it to the other party; when the tx_commit() function called by the dequeuing process returns successfully, it means the message has been removed from the queue.

The TMQFORWARD server provides a service that dequeues a message and passes them to a service, therefore providing a mechanism to call a service using a queue. One common use of an application queue is for storing requests and then using TMQFORWARD to forward them to a service routine. Also, online service requests that failed can be enqueued in an application queue for later processing.

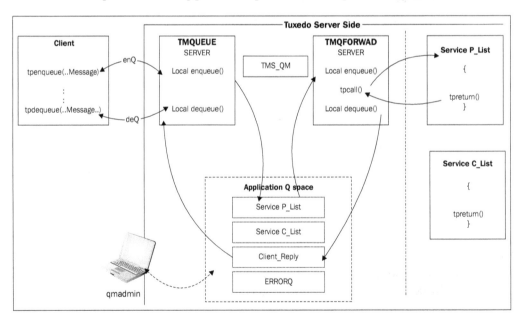

The syntax for the `tpenqueue` and `tpdequeue` function is as follows (you also need to include `<atmi.h>`):

- `tpenqueue()` – `int tpenqueue(char *q-space, char *q-name, TPQCTL *ctlptr, char *indata, long length, long flags)`
- `tpdequeue()` – `int tpdequeue(char *q-space, char *q-name, TPQCTL *ctlptr, char **indata, long *length, long flags)`

The `flags` value can be set using one of these four different ways: TPNOTRAN, TPNOBLOCK, TPNOTIME, and TPSIGRSTRT.

Event-based communication

So far we have discussed the request/response communication paradigm and using a queue for communication, but many times we may be required to handle unexpected real-world events that, if not properly handled, may affect the business. Tuxedo basically offers two kinds of event-based communications, **unsolicited client notification** and the **event-broker server**.

Unsolicited notifications are used to communicate with the client. Tuxedo provides two mechanisms to manage these simple events: **single-program** notifications and **multiple-program** broadcasting. These help to communicate unsolicited notifications to the clients only, as the servers are designed to receive solicited communication in the form of service requests. The `tpnotify()` function is used to send an unsolicited message to another client. The CLIENTID parameter is the ID for a client, data is the message to be passed, len is the length, and the flags parameters are TPNOBLOCK, TPNOTIME, or TPSIGRSTRT. On the other hand, `tpbroadcast()` is used to send a message to all or a group of clients by using the first three parameters (LMID, USERNAME, and CLIENTID); setting null values for these make them wildcards. The rest of the three parameters are all the same as `tppost()`. A client uses `tpsetunsol()` to register a callback function to get the unsolicited notification.

The Tuxedo event-broker server provides the capability for posting messages, which are received by the processes that have subscribed to it. A process (server or client) can subscribe to an event with a name or set a rule to prescribe event subscription. We should remember that the event-broker server should be used to handle exceptional cases, but not as a normal communication mechanism for passing messages.

The following are the characteristics of the Tuxedo event-broker server:

- The server or a client can post or subscribe to an event
- The same event can be posted by many processes and vice versa
- Tuxedo provides a set of system event that can be subscribed to by a client or server

Tuxedo provides an event-broker server called TMUSREVT. It helps to store the subscription information as tpsubscribe() is being called; similarly, tppost() invokes it to post an event for the subscriber(s). In the case of unsolicited subscription, this server creates a message using tppost() and sends an unsolicited message to the clients that subscribed to that unsolicited event. Let us look at how we can subscribe, post, and unsubscribe from an event:

- Subscribe to an event by name using the tpsubscribe() function. The event-expr argument is the name of one or more events, filterptr is the rule to select the specific event, ctlptr is the pointer to an event-control structure (it is NULL for unsolicited notifications), and the flags parameter is TPEVSERVICE, TPEVQUEUE, TPEVTRAN, or TPEVPERSIST. The tpsubscribe() function returns a handler for a specific subscription, which should be used for unsubscription.

  tpsubscribe – long tpsubscribe (char *event-expr, char *filterptr, TPEVCTL *ctlptr, long flags)

- Post (initiate or notify) an event by using tppost(). It posts an event identified by event-name; indata is the message you would like to pass to its subscriber(s), length is the message length, and flags can have values TPSIGRSTRT, TPNOTRAN, TPNOREPLY, TPNOBLOCK, and TPNOTIME.

  tppost – tppost(char *event-name, char *indata, long length, long flags)

- Unsubscribe from the event by using tpunsubscribe(). The subscription is a valid handler returned by tpsubscribe(). A client must use this function before it calls tpterm().

  tpunsubscribe –int tpunsubscribe (long subscription-name, long flags)

So, there are two ways to use event-based communication, namely unsolicited client notification by using the tpnotify() and tpbroadcast() functions, and event-broker server by using the tppost() and tpsubscribe() functions.

Transaction in Tuxedo

This is one of the most important sections in client/server architecture. The foundation of Tuxedo ATMI is a proven, reliable transaction processor, also known as a Transaction Processing (TP) monitor. This transaction processing has very unique characteristics consisting **Atomicity**, **Consistency**, **Isolation**, and **Durability**, also known as **ACID**.

- **Atomicity**: All changes to data are committed in a single operation, which means all the changes are done at once, otherwise they are rolled back

- **Consistency**: This means that the data has to be in a consistent state before and after the transaction

- **Isolation**: This means that transactions run concurrently and appear to be serialized; the intermediate state of a transaction is unseen to other transactions

- **Durability**: Once a transaction is committed, the changes to data should be saved and cannot be lost, even in the event of a system failure

The XA interface and two-phase commit

In a real-life scenario, we need to have a single function that needs to update or insert the data in multiple resources (of multiple databases or file systems). To achieve this, one needs to use a **Distributed Transaction Processing** (DTP) model. The **eXtended Architecture** (**XA**) standard defines the two-phase commit protocol that helps to achieve this challenging task. The XA was originally conceived in the Tuxedo project and has been standardized by the X/Open Company, Ltd., an independent, worldwide, open-system organization supported by most IT organizations in the world. In this scenario, a communication between a transaction manager (TM) and a resource manager (RM) is done through APIs based on Tuxedo XA. An RM is a system service (for example, database system) that manages durable data. A TM manages distributed transactions, which may span multiple resource managers. It manages a two-phase commit (to maintain the ACID properties), which involves coordination among multiple resource managers to commit distributed transactions, or it rolls them back if one of them fails to commit, and instead coordinates failure recovery.

In a Tuxedo-based application, the Tuxedo system plays both the role of TM and RM. We have discussed a Tuxedo queue as a reliable messaging queue, as it uses this XA standard to make the queue-based messaging "ACIDic" in nature, where the application's queuing manager is an RM.

In Tuxedo, a TM does the following for a transaction:

- Creates a global transaction identifier (GTI) when the application initiates a transaction

- Tracks all the participants (RMs) of the transaction

- The TM notifies the RM with GTI during communication

- Performs the two-phase commit, which means communication for phase-1 (preparation and ready) and phase-2 for the commit

- It performs the rollback process if the application designates that the transaction is to be aborted

- It performs a recovery procedure when failures occur

Creating or initiating a transaction

There are mainly two ways to initiate a transaction in a Tuxedo system: initiated explicitly by the application, or implicitly by an administrator.

- In your application code, you can use the `tpbegin()` function to initiate your transaction. It creates the GTI and starts the transaction and communicates it to the TM. This function has two parameters: a transaction time-out value and a flag, which is currently undefined and must be set to 0. The application module that called `tpbegin()` should also call a termination-of-transaction function, `tpcommit()` to commit, or `tpabort()` to abort the transaction.

- The Tuxedo system provides a built-in administrative configuration option called AUTOTRAN. The service that is marked with it in the UBBCONFIG file is part of a global transaction of its caller. If it is not being called under a transaction, the Tuxedo system initiates the transaction prior to invoking this service.

Tuxedo's transactional functions

The following is a list of Tuxedo's transactional functions along with their syntax:

- `tpbegin` – `int tpbegin(unsigned long timeout, long flags)`
- `tpcommit` – `int tpcommit(long flags)`
- `tpabort` – `int tpabort(long flags)`
- `tpgetlev` – `int tpgetlev()`
- `tpsuspend` – `int tpsuspend(TPTRANID *t_id, long flags)`
- `tpresume` – `int tpresume(TPTRANID *t_id, long flags)`
- `tpopen` – `int tpopen(void)`
- `tpclose` – `int tpclose(void)`

Tuxedo Transaction Log (TLOG)

The Tuxedo system saves information about all the participants in a transaction for tracking in the TLOG (Transaction LOG). The information (the reply from the global transaction participants) for a global transaction is stored in the TLOG file during the process of being committed. The TLOG holds the record for a global transaction that needs to be committed. The TLOG doesn't hold any records for transactions that need to be rolled back. Please make sure you create the **Universal Device List** (**UDL**) by using the following command:

```
tmadmin -c crdl  -z "full path of device" -b "block size to be allocated"
for using TLOG.
```

Also, you must set the TLOGNAME, TLOGDEVICE, TLOGSIZEE, and TLOGOFFSET parameters in the MACHINES section of the UBBCONFIG file. You can create the TLOG in a filesystem or by using the Oracle database.

Summary

In this chapter, we have discussed various Tuxedo ATMI interfaces to develop our client/server application using different types of Tuxedo buffers, as well as various communication patterns such as request/reply, conversational, queue-based, and event-based communication. The event-based communication can be of two types: unsolicited client notification and event-broker server. It should not be used as a normal communication protocol, and should be used rather to handle an exception. We also discussed XA transactions and how to communicate in transactional mode in such a way that we are able to maintain data integrity and persistence.

4
SALT – Service Architecture Leveraging Tuxedo

In this chapter, we will discuss **Service Architecture Leveraging Tuxedo** (**SALT**). The Service Oriented Architecture (SOA) has been proven in the industry today, and SALT was introduced to make the Tuxedo application an integral part of the SOA environment. By looking at the Tuxedo architecture, we can certainly claim that Tuxedo is one of the oldest forms of SOA platforms. Everything in Tuxedo is a service and invoked as a service, and they are very loosely coupled. It is known for its performance, scalability, and reliability. The SCA-based (**Service Component Architecture**) development provides us with a more complete SOA solution, and with SALT we can connect with the Tuxedo framework, enabling the re-use of its services and giving a better ROI. SALT is a Tuxedo add-on product; one of its components is the SCA container, which enables any applications based on web services to call Tuxedo services and vice versa. The other component is a native web-service stack.

Getting acquainted with SALT

SALT enables Tuxedo users to expose Tuxedo-based services as web services to ensure that any external web-service-based application can call a Tuxedo service just like calling another web service. Also, SALT helps Tuxedo applications to call external web services without any code development.

SALT is an integral solution for a Tuxedo application and web services, and it enables seamless integration between Tuxedo applications and external web-service-based applications. It increases the possibility of SOA adoption for any organization with distributed applications spanning over large physical distances with diverse hardware and software platforms. So, you can use SALT to extend your Tuxedo application in a more loosely coupled manner and re-use and protect your ROI.

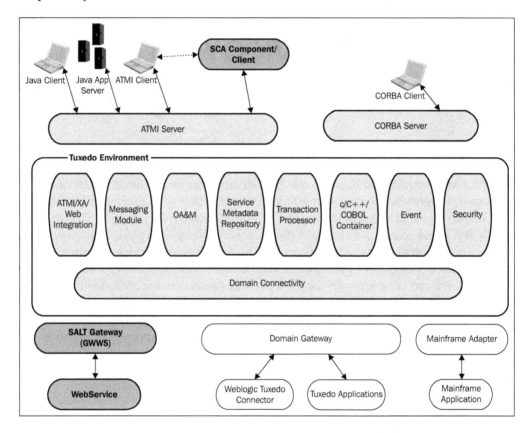

To use SALT, we need to know its components and some of the important concepts behind it. Let us look at them in detail.

The SALT gateway (GWWS) and service metadata repository server

The **SALT gateway** (GWWS) is a Tuxedo server that works as an adapter to communicate with other web service applications using a SOAP over an HTTP/S protocol. Like all other Tuxedo system servers, the GWWS server needs to be configured in the UBBCONFIG file and works bi-directionally (inbound/outbound). It issues a native Tuxedo service call as it gets a SOAP request over an HTTP/S. On the other hand, it also takes the Tuxedo requests and issues the SOAP calls to external web-service applications. The **Tuxedo service metadata repository** provides Tuxedo's service contract information to GWWS during its boot time. It also gets the SALT-related information from the configuration file. This GWWS server also works like a web server and provides simple functionalities such as downloading the WSDL or XML file. The service metadata repository server called TMMETADATA (also a Tuxedo-provided server) has a service called TMMETAREPOS to process requests or to retrieve or update the Tuxedo service metadata repository information.

WSDL utilities for SALT

There are two utilities that come with SALT. The first one is tmwsdlgen, which helps to generate SCA, SCDL, and server-side interface files for Tuxedo services. The second one is wsdlcvt, a WSDL converter to ensure that a Tuxedo services can be exposed as a web service using SALT. This WSDL document can be used to integrate the Tuxedo service as a web service. This wsdlcvt utility takes WSDL as an input and converts it to a definition file for Tuxedo. The GWWS server utilizes the SALT deployment file, which needs to be imported from SALT's web service definition file. On the other hand, interface information for Tuxedo client programming is provided by the Tuxedo service metadata repository's definition file and the FML32 field table definition file.

The SCA concept and Tuxedo service

There is a trend in the IT industry today of organizations moving from application-centric architecture to service-oriented architecture (SOA). SOA is all about building the functionality of an application by using a set of services or components stitched together (called a **work flow**), to ensure that they meet certain end-to-end business needs. The SCA models have a standard guideline, which basically gives recommendations on how to build and implement services, the mechanism of reusing services, and how to accumulate or constitute services into solutions so that your SOA implementation is more efficient and flexible. The SCA model helps you with service deployment and constructing and assembling a service prior to its deployment.

In SCA, components can be built in various standard languages and can be deployed in the related container. You may access them using various standard methods. So, a component provides some business functions that can be published as a service. The implementation can have dependencies on the services of other components, which can be accessed through references. Each of these components can have properties, which can be set using an XML file. So, multiple components can be joined logically to provide an e2e business solution; in an SCA model, these are known as **composites**. As an example, a composite may contain one or more components connected through a reference (for example, under the WebLogic environment). SALT provides mechanisms to use a Tuxedo service as one of the components of a composite or business solution.

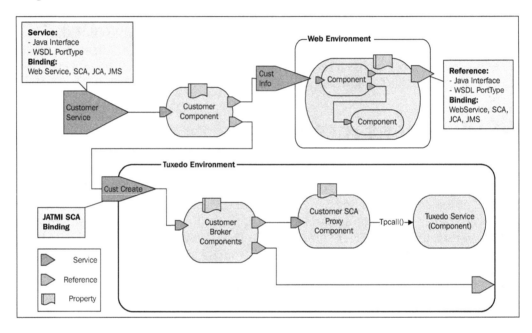

In this section, we have briefly gone through the major components and concepts of SALT. This basic knowledge will help us configure and build a SALT application, which is explained in the following sections.

SALT installation

As we discussed earlier, SALT is an accompanying product for Tuxedo, and it can be installed in the same three ways as Tuxedo—GUI-based, console-based, and silent installation. The SALT executable comes as an installer file. You can execute it on Windows or Unix platforms using various methods.

The SALT distribution contains the following components, which get installed under the TUXDIR directory:

- SALT service component architecture support
- SALT web service gateway server software
- SALT web service development assistant utilities
- SALT administrative utilities
- SALT sample applications

A supported version of Tuxedo must be installed before you install SALT; you need the correct compatible versions of Tuxedo and SALT to work together. If you already have the Tuxedo server installed, you can install the SALT client and/or server, and of course, the server-side sample applications. On the other hand, you can only install the SALT client component if you have the Tuxedo client.

GUI-based installation

For SALT's GUI-based installation on Windows or on Unix, you need to carry out the steps pointed out in the following sections.

Installing on Windows

Carry out the following steps for SALT's GUI-based installation on Windows:

1. Go to **Run** on the **Start** menu.
2. Select the Windows installer executable file, salt11gR1_tux11gR1_32_win2k8_x86_vs2008.exe.
3. Click on **Open**.
4. InstallAnywhere runs and the **Introduction** screen appears.
5. Click on **NEXT** to proceed with the installation. The rest of the steps are very user friendly and self-explanatory; just make sure the home directory is properly chosen.

Installing on Unix

Log in as a root, or another user with sufficient permissions, and perform the following steps:

1. Execute the installation program. For example:

   ```
   UNIXPrompt> sh salt11gR1_tux11gR1_64_hpux_1123_ia.bin
   ```

2. The **Introduction** screen will appear. Click on **Next** to proceed with the installation. The rest of the steps are very user friendly and self-explanatory; just make sure the home directory is properly chosen.

Console-based installation

SALT's console-based installation is only for Unix; follow the ensuing steps:

1. Log in as a root or any other user with sufficient permissions.

2. Execute the installation program. For example, for the HP-UX platform, select either of the following:

    ```
    UNIXPrompt> # salt11gR1_tux11gR1_64_hpux_1123_ia.bin -i console
    ```

    Or

    ```
    ./salt11gR1_tux11gR1_64_hpux_1123_ia.bin -i console
    ```

3. The installation program runs and prompts you for responses (see the *the Listing 3-1* section at `http://docs.oracle.com/cd/E15261_01/salt/ docs11gr1/install/instcon.html#wp1036651` for an example).

4. `InstallAnywhere` will guide you through the installation. So, just follow the instructions and you will get a completion message once you are done with the installation.

Silent installation

For silent-mode installation, you need to create a template file; they are different for Unix and Windows. Please refer to following URL for more details on silent-mode installation:

`http://docs.oracle.com/cd/E15261_01/salt/docs11gr1/install/instsil. html`

In this section, we have gone through the various installation processes for SALT on Windows and Unix systems. As a post-installation task, you may consider verifying SALT's directory structure; for example, you will find all the utilities/functions (previously listed) under the `/bin` directory. Similarly, there will be some header files (`ws*`, `SCA`, and `SOA`) under the `/include` directory, and so on.

Configuration of a SALT application

In the previous sections, we have discussed the various components of SALT and how to install them; now we will discuss how to configure these components in brief. In this configuration section, we will touch base on most of the important components of SALT; for example, Tuxedo web services, Tuxedo SCA components, service contract discovery, and SALT WS-TX support.

SCA container APIs and utilities

In this section, we will discuss SALT's command-line utilities and some of the functions. Some of the most commonly used commands are explained in detail here.

The buildscaclient command

The `buildscaclient` command is used to build a client program to call SCA-based components running on the Tuxedo environment.

```
buildscaclient -c default_component [-v] [-h] [-k] [-o name] [-s SCAroot]
[-f firstfiles] [-l lastfiles] [-S structurefiles]
```

The following are the attributes of this command:

- `-c` – This specifies the component to be used for this application
- `-v` – This is a pacifier to turn off/on the verbose mode of this command
- `-k` – This is to maintain the generated proxy files that allow dynamic interfacing of clients and references
- `-o` – This is the name of the client application generated by this command
- `-s` – The location of the SCA root where the required components are located (the SCDL files)
- `-f` – This is used to include the files first (before the SCA libraries) during the compile time of this command
- `-l` – This is used to include the files last during compile time of this command
- `-S` – A source or binary file that specifies the SCA structure

The buildscacomponent command

The buildscacomponent command is used to build the SCA components from the SCDL source file where the component(s) in the composite(s) file(s) is(are) specified, and it then produces equivalent executable libraries.

```
buildscacomponent [-v] [-s scaroot] [-f firstfiles] [-l lastfiles] [-S
structurefiles] -c compositename[/componentname]
[,compositename,..]] [-y] [-k] [-h]
```

The following are the attributes of this command:

- -v – This is a pacifier to turn off/on the verbose mode of this command
- -s – The location of the SCA root where the required components are located (SCDL files)
- -f – This is used to include a file first (before the SCA libraries) during compile time
- -l – This is used to include a file at the last during compile time of this command
- -c – This specifies the name of the composite(s) processed
- -K – This is used to retain the generated proxy and wrapper source
- -S – A source or binary file that specifies the SCA structure

The buildscaserver command

The buildscaserver command is used to create a Tuxedo server from the SCDL definitions and interfaces.

```
buildscaserver -o servername -wp1160640 composite[,composite] [-v] [-s
scaroot] [-w] [-r rmname] [-y] [-k] [-t] [-S]
```

The following are the attributes of this command:

- -o – This specifies the executable name of the server
- -c – This specifies the list of the composite(s) hosted
- -v – This is a pacifier to turn off/on the verbose mode of this command
- -s – The location of the SCA root where the required components are located (the SCDL files)
- -w – This specifies that the generated server will host the web-service, binding-enabled components
- -r – This specifies the resource manager (RM) attached with this server

- -k – This is to retain the server's main stub
- -t – This flag is not used in the current release
- -s – This is required if you use the C-structure input or output buffers in the server or if you use the -w option

The GWWS command

The Tuxedo system provides a web service gateway server, and like all other Tuxedo servers, it needs to be configured in the UBBCONFIG file.

```
GWWS SRVGRP="identifier" SRVID=number [other_parms] CLOPT="-A -- - i
InstanceID"
```

Here, the -i option is to identify the GWWS server with an exclusive ID; it is required to differentiate when you have more than one GWWS server in the same Tuxedo environment. So, this identifier needs to be exclusive with all GWWS servers in the UBBCONFIG file.

The following table lists the rest of the SALT-related functions and utilities along with their descriptions and the syntax you need to know to use SALT along with the commands we discussed previously:

Command/function()	Syntax	Comments
mkfldfromschema and mkfld32from schema	mkfldfromschema [{-i schema|-u schemaurl}] [-b basenumber]]-o outputfile]	The mkfldfromschema/ mkfld32fromschema command takes an XML schema and creates a field table; the options are the same for both commands.
mkviewfromschema and mkview32from schema	mkviewfromschema [{-i schema|-u schemaurl}] [-o outputfile]	The mkviewfromschema/ mkview32fromschema command takes an XML schema and creates a view file; the options are the same for both commands.
scaadmin	scaadmin -v {for verbose}	This is the SCA server management command interpreter. It has multiple options for monitoring or changing the SCA components hosted in the Tuxedo environment. Use help all for all the options available.

Command/function()	Syntax	Comments
SCAHOST	SCAHOST SRVGRP="identifier" SRVID="number" CLOPT="[-A] [servopts options] -- -w -c composite"	The Tuxedo server needs information from the metadata repository, so you need to specify this in the UBBCONFIG file on the TMMETADATA system process.
scapasswordtool	scapasswordstore -i passwordidentifier -[a|d]	This is to encrypt a password and store it in a file that is used by SCA components to refer to Tuxedo-based services. You can also use this to delete the password.
scastructc32 and scastructc	scastructc32 [-n] [-d viewdir] structfile [structfile . . .]	This works like a compiler for the structure's description; it takes the structure's description file as input and creates an equivalent binary file (which is interpreted at runtime to determine data mapping between the FML buffers and C++ structures) and multiple header files.
scastructdis32 and scastructdis	scastructdis32 [-E envlabel] viewobjfile [viewobjfile...]	This produces and displays view information in the view file's format from a binary file, which is created using scastructc32 or viewc32.
scatuxgen	scatuxgen (-c <composite file name> | -i <interface file name> [-I <inbuf>] [-O <outbuf>])-s <service name> [-t <string-type>] [-w [-n <namespace> -a <network address>]] [-v]	This parses the SCDL file and creates metadata repository interface information that is based on SCA's abstract class.
setSCAPassword Callback()	#include <tuxsca.h>void setSCAPasswordCallback (char * (_ TMDLLENTRY *)(*disp) (char*identifier))	This is the function that allows you to get the password dynamically.

Command/function()	Syntax	Comments
tmscd	tmscd start|stop|status [-e] [-f <file>][id1 [id2 [...]]]	This command activates and deactivates service contract discovery.
tmwsdlgen	tmwsdlgen - c wsdf_file [-y] [-o wsdl_file] [-m {pack|raw|mtom}] [-t{wls|axis}]	This helps to create a WSDL document (this has been discussed previously).
tuxscagen	tuxscagen [-s <target-root-directory>] [-d <service-name>] [-C <TUXEDO_cltname>] [-u <TUXEDO_username>] [(-S | -j <java_package_name>)] [-o <output_SCDL_filename>] [-i <output_interface_filename>[-m <max-intf-arguments>] [-y] [-v] [-F] [-c] [-h] [-g<i|a|s>] [-trepository=<filename> | -tinfile=<metarepos. infile> | -tmetadata]	This helps to create SCA, SCDL, and server-side interface files for Tuxedo services (this has been discussed previously).
wsadmin	wsadmin [-v]	This is the administrative command for the GWWS server, which helps you to monitor this process. Use help with this command for a list of commands.
wsdlcvt	wsdlcvt -i WSDL_URL -o output_basename [-m] [-v] [-y] [-w] [-sh] [-sp]	This command converts the WSDL document to a metadata-input file, FML32 mapping file, and a SALT Web Service Definition file (WSDF).
wsloadcf	wsloadcf [-n] [-y] [-D loglevel] saltdeploy_file	This creates a binary SALTCONFIG file from the SALT deployment file and other referenced artifacts.

Configuring the Tuxedo web services

In this section, we will discuss most of the web-services-related configuration to set up your SALT environment, such as the UBBCONFIG file, the Tuxedo metadata repository, configuring native or external web services, the deployment file, and compiling the SALT configuration.

The UBBCONFIG file

We all know the importance of the UBBCONFIG file for a Tuxedo application. To incorporate SALT in your application, you need to include some entries for SALT components in this file; some of them are musts and some of them are optional, as described here:

- **The TMMETADATA server in the *SERVERS section** (required): TMMETADATA is the server provided by Tuxedo. It has the TMMETAREPOS service, which processes requests to retrieve or update the Tuxedo service metadata repository information. For example:

  *SERVERS

  TMMETADATA

  SRVGRP=MyGrp SRVID=202 RESTART=Y MAXGEN=4

  GRACE=2500 CLOPT="-A -- -f /usr/MyApps/Metadata"

- **The GWWS servers in the *SERVERS section** (required): This is the web service gateway server that we discussed a couple of times. The GWWS server refers to the SALTCONFIG file during boot up, so the environment variable SALTCONFIG must be set prior to starting up this GWWS server. Also, the TMMETADATA server should be booted up before GWWS, because this server calls the services of TMMETADATA. One or more GWWS servers can be configured in the same Tuxedo domain, but each GWWS server must have a unique instance ID using the -i option. For example:

  *SERVERS

  GWWS

  SRVGRP= MyGrp   SRVID=210

      SEC_PRINCIPAL_NAME="gwws_ PASSWD "   optional(#4 points below)

      SEC_PRINCIPAL_PASSVAR="gwws_PASSWD"   optional(#4 points below)

      CLOPT="-A -- - i MyGWWS1"

- **Parameters in the UBBCONFIG file** (required): You need to consider MAXSERVERS, MAXSERVICES, and MAXACCESSERS in the RESOURCES section of UBBCONFIG as you start adding the GWWS and TMMETADATA servers. Also, you need to consider MAXWSCLIENTS under the MACHINES section, as GWWS inbound-communication connectivity for web services is controlled by this variable.

- **Certificate a password phrase for the GWWS servers** (optional): To set SSL link-level encryption for GWWS, you need to configure a certificate password.

- **Configuring Tuxedo authentication for web service clients** (optional): To check the validity of the web service's clients, SALT's GWWS servers leverage the Tuxedo authentication framework. So, the client has to send the user credentials through the SOAP/HTTP message header.

- **Configuring the Tuxedo security level for outbound HTTP basic authentication** (optional): The USER_AUTH, ACL, or MANDATORY_ACL options can be defined in the UBBCONFIG file and in the Tuxedo client's uid/gid for outbound HTTP basic authentication username/password mapping.

The Tuxedo service metadata repository

As we previously discussed, the service metadata repository is a collection of Tuxedo service characteristics that are particularly useful in clarifying the request/response details of a Tuxedo service. The GWWS depends on the Tuxedo service metadata repository for communication between the Tuxedo request/response format and the standard message of type SOAP. Here we will discuss some important command-line utilities provided by Tuxedo that are used to configure or monitor the metadata repository. Some of these utilities are briefly described in the previous table.

- **tmloadrepos**: This is the command-line tool that produces or updates the metadata repository binary file and loads it with the service parameter information.

  ```
  Prompt> tmloadrepos [-e|-d service1[,...]] [-y] [-i repository_
  input file] repository_file
  ```

  The input file contains the service information you need to run with tmloadrepos to create the binary file; an example of the file is as follows:

  ```
  service=Ballance
  svcdescription=This service returns account Balance
  export=Y
  inbuf=FML
  outbuf=FML
  ```

```
param=ACCOUNT_ID

type=string

paramdescription=Account ID

access=in

count=2

requiredcount=2


param=BALANCE

paramdescription=The Balance value.

type=integer

access=out

count=2

requiredcount=2
```

- **tmunloadrepos**: This displays the file service information from the Tuxedo service metadata repository.

  ```
  Prompt> tmunloadrepos [-s service_regular_expression1[,...]] [-t|-c] repository file
  ```

  The -t option is for a text file and -c is for C pseudocode options, and they are mutually exclusive.

- **tpgetrepos**: This function uses the FML32 buffer to get service information from the metadata repository dynamically.

  ```
  int tpgetrepos(char *reposfile, FBFR32* idata, FBFR32** odata)
  ```

- **tpsetrepos**: This function also uses the FML32 buffer to set the add, update, or delete information on the service parameter in the metadata repository file dynamically.

  ```
  int tpsetrepos(char *reposfile, FBFR32* idata, FBFR32** odata)
  ```

This metadata repository is one of the most important components in SALT; we have discussed the most important and basic steps for it. There are many other operations and options available that will help you to administrate this repository on a larger scale. Please refer to the following URL for more information about this:

```
http://docs.oracle.com/cd/E15261_01/salt/docs11gr1/admin/config.html#wp1093834
```

Configuration of the native web services

This is done to expose a Tuxedo service as a web service to the outer world; there are mainly three steps to do this:

1. **Creating a native WSDF**: A native WSDF is needed to expose a Tuxedo service as a web service through the HTTP/S endpoints. Please consider the following steps; we have picked up the `simapp` application as an example:

    1. **Configuring the SOAP header**: The `wssoapflds.h` file comes with SALT, and it is where you find the `mapsoapheader` attribute to configure SOAP headers. `False` is the default for this parameter, which means that the GWWS server does not do any mapping between the FML fields and the SOAP header.

    2. **Configuring the WSBinding object**: The `<WSBinding>` element needs to have a unique WSBinding ID in the WSDF. So, the `SALTDEPLOY` file, which gets referred by the GWWS server, is the required indicator of the `WSBinding` object.

    3. **Configuring the service object**: The `<Service>` element is basically the name of the Tuxedo service to be published.

    4. **Configuring the message conversion handler**: To modify the SOAP XML payload and the Tuxedo buffer types, convert the routine to fit your own plugins. For more information on this, refer to Oracle's SALT user manual. For example:

        ```
        <Definition ...>
          <WSBinding id="simapp_binding">
            <Servicegroup id="simapp">
              <Service name="toupper" />
                <Property name="mapsoapheader" value="true" />
                  </Service>
                </Servicegroup>
              <SOAP version="1.2" style="rpc" use="encoded">
                  <AccessingPoints>
                    ...
                  </AccessingPoints>
              </SOAP>
          </WSBinding>
        </Definition>
        ```

2. **Using the WS-Policy files**: To use advanced features (such as reliable messaging or web-service message-level security), you may need to configure the WS-Policy files.

3. **Generating a WSDL file from a native WSDF**: You need to use `tmwsdlgen` on WSDF to create a WSDL file; for example:

```
Prompt> tmwsdlgen -c MyApp.wsdf -o MyApp.wsdl
```

So, in this section, we have briefly discussed the steps to expose Tuxedo services as web services.

Configuration of external web services

Tuxedo can invoke an external web service, and to do that you need to carry out the following steps:

1. **Converting a WSDL file into Tuxedo definitions**: The command `wsdlcvt` is a wrapper script that provides a user friendly WSDL converter interface.

```
Prompt> wsdlcvt -i ExWebService.wsdl -o tuxDefinition
```

The following files are created by this tool:

   ° **Oracle Tuxedo service metadata repository input file**: The GWWS server refers to the repository and advertises SALT's proxy services to ensure that they will be recognized by any ATMI call from a Tuxedo service.

   ° **FML32 field table definition file**: This is just a data-mapping mechanism between the Tuxedo `FML32` buffer and a WSDL message.

   ° **Non-native WSDF file**: A WSDF file needs to be deployed for the GWWS server to work as an outbound connector; you need to create this WSDF file from the WSDL file using a `wsdlcvt` converter.

   ° **XML schema file**: The WSDL and XML (embedded or imported) files used by GWWS servers are saved as `.xsd` under the same file directory.

2. **Post conversion tasks**: Tools do most of the work for you, but during conversion, some naming conflicts may occur, so you need to be careful about data points and their correctness:

   The following is the naming convention for SALT's proxy service definitions:

   ° Removing the duplicated name of the service in the metadata keyword (`tuxservice`) definitions

   ° Removing the duplicated field names in the `FML32` buffer definitions

3. **How to load SALT proxy service metadata definitions**: You need to run `tmloadrepos` to load the SALT proxy service metadata definitions into the service metadata repository once you have resolved all naming conflicts.

4. **Environment variables for GWWS runtime**: Please make sure your environment variables FLDTBLDIR32 and FIELDTBLS32 are set accordingly. You may set these two environment variables already if you are using an existing environment. Also, you need to set XSDDIR and XSDFILES accordingly to access all the XML schema(s) under one directory.

The SALTDEPLOY file is an XML-type file and is used for SALT deployments. This is to define SALT's GWWS server deployment data, which is based on each Tuxedo environment (machine). It takes care of three basic tasks:

- Lists all the necessary Web Service Definition files (WSDF)

- Defines the number of GWWS servers that are deployed on a Tuxedo machine

- Associates endpoint access for each inbound or outbound web service

The following is an example of the SALTDEPLOY file format:

```
<Deployment xmlns="…">
   <WSDF>
         <Import location="…" />            Zero or more entry
   </WSDF>
  <WSGateway>
     <GWInstance id="…">                 Zero or more entry
         <Inbound>                       Zero or one entry
           <Binding ref="…">             Zero or more entry
               <Endpoint use="…"/>       One or more entry
           </Binding>
       </Inbound>
       <Outbound>                        Zero or more entry
           <Binding ref="… "/>           Zero or more entry
             <WSAddressing="… "/>        Zero or one entry
                 <Endpoint use="…"/>     Zero or more entry
       </Outbound>
       <TLogDevice>                      Zero or more entry
       <TLogName>                        Zero or more entry
       <WSATEndPoint>                    Zero or more entry
       <MaxTran>                         Zero or more entry
       <Properties>                      Zero or one entry
  <Property="… "/>                       Zero or more entry
       </Properties>
     </GWInstance>
   </WSGateway>
<System>
   <Certificate>                         Zero or one entry
       <PrivateKey>"…" </PrivateKey>
```

```
        <VerifyClient "…"/>                  Zero or one entry
    </Certificate>
    <Plugin>                                 Zero or one entry
        <Interface library="…" />            Zero or more entry
    </Plugin>
</Deployment>
```

The previous SALTDEPLOY file format example gives you detailed information on this file, which is a major input for the web service application in the binary SALTCONFIG file.

To create a SALTDEPLOY file, carry out the following steps:

1. **Import the WSDF files**: You need to import your WSDF file to a SALT deployment file; make sure the name is a unique WSDF name, as it's required by the GWWS servers to make deployment relations.

2. **Set up the GWWS servers**: Multiple outbound or inbound objects (WSBindin) can be defined in the WSDF file, which is used during deployment. For each inbound object, there should be one access endpoint as an inbound endpoint; on the other hand, for an outbound endpoint, there can be zero or more access endpoints. These endpoints are from the list of WSBinding objects.

3. **Set up system-level resources**: In SALT, all global resources shared by all the GWWS servers are defined in the SALTDEPLOY file. The certificate and libraries for the plugins for the system-level resources need to be configured in this file; please refer to the previous example.

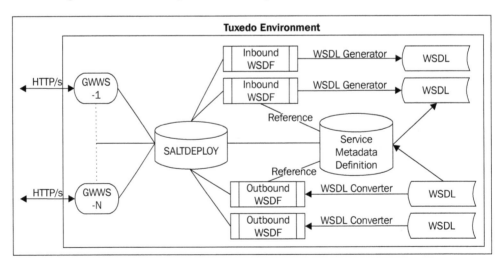

In this section, we have briefly discussed the structure of the deployment file and how to configure its major components. There are some advanced options for SALT; for example, security, configuring advanced web-service messaging, and SALT in MP mode. For more information on these topics, you may refer to the following URL:

```
http://docs.oracle.com/cd/E15261_01/salt/docs11gr1/ref/deploy.html
```

Compiling the SALT configuration

We have learned how to create the XML-based deployment file, SALTDEPLOY, for the GWWS server. The command wsloadcf takes the SALTDEPLOY file and the WSDF file to crosscheck with the WS-Policy to validate the syntax according to the XML schema of each file format, and it then loads a binary configuration file called SALTCONFIG. The command wsloadcf validates the SALT deployment file according to the XML schema files, which stay in the $TUXDIR/udataobj/salt path (under your Tuxedo/ SALT installation folder).

```
Prompt> wsloadcf [-n] [-y] [-D loglevel] saltdeploy_file
```

The wsloadcf command can be executed to validate SALTDEPLOY without generating the binary version using the -n option.

Configuring SCA components

There are seven different SCA components for Tuxedo; we will briefly discuss how to configure them in this book, but for a detailed example, please refer to the following URL:

```
http://docs.oracle.com/cd/E15261_01/salt/docs11gr1/admin/config.
html#wp1095184
```

SCA ATMI client configuration

The SCA ATMI client is a native Tuxedo client that you build by following the SCA model and compile using the buildscaclient command utility. This client program should stay in the same directory where the root.composite file is located; the path of this file should be included in the APPDIR environment variable.

SCA JATMI client configuration

This is the composite file and part of the Java `.jar` file for the JATMI client, located at the base of the `.jar` file. The Java runtime loads the composite file when the application is run. The `CLASSPATH` variable should be set with the client application `.jar` file along with `binding-jatmi-extension.jar`, `com.oracle.jatmi.dataxfm_1.0.0.0.jar`, `com.bea.core.jatmi_1.2.0.3.jar`, `tuscany-sca-manifest.jar`, and `com.bea.core.i18n_1.4.0.0.jar`.

SCA workstation client configuration

The configuration of the SCA WS clients is similar to the SCA native clients we previously discussed; the difference is that you need to have the `<workStationParameters>` element and its subelements in the composite. The SCA runtime automatically detects whether the client is built as an SCA native client or an SCA WS client, and it loads the correct reference binding library accordingly. The environment variable `$APPDIR` needs to point to the client's application directory.

SCA web service client configuration

The SCA web service client uses the `<binding.ws>` element, unlike the SCA native client, which uses `<binding.atmi>`. The environment variable `$APPDIR` needs to be pointed to the client's application directory.

The appropriate proxy stub needs to be built in `<interface.cpp>`. The WSDL file needs to be in the client directory where the endpoints are defined in the `<binding.ws>` element. Also, you need to carry out the following steps for configuring the GWWS server:

1. Shutdown TMMETADATA and GWWS if they are up and running.
2. Run `wsdlcvt` on the WSDL to produce a WSDF file, a Tuxedo metadata repository interface definitions file, the FML32 field tables, and XML schemas.
3. Check and update (if needed) the WSDF file for the correct endpoint address used at runtime.
4. Run `tmloadrepos` to load the interface definitions into the TMMETADATA server from the Tuxedo metadata repository.
5. Alter the reference to the WSDF file in the configuration input file for GWWS.
6. Run `wsloadcf` to reload the binary configuration file for GWWS.
7. Reboot GWWS and TMMETADATA.

SCA ATMI server configuration

For the SCA ATMI server, you need one composite file that defines the SCA application. During runtime, it loads all the composite and component-type files for SCA server applications that are running on a Tuxedo environment. The $APPDIR variable is the SCA root, the same as that for the SCA ATMI server.

SCA web service server configuration

The configuration of the web services binding for components is similar to the ATMI binding for hosting SCA components. The SCA component needs to be built using the buildscaserver command with the -w option (web services) to be hosted in the Tuxedo application. Just as a reminder, this server needs to have an entry under the *SERVERS section of UBBCONFIG.

Also, the GWWS configuration has to be incorporated with the same changes; follow the same seven steps mentioned previously for SCA web service client configuration to do this.

SCA client security configuration

The SCA components of Tuxedo leverage Tuxedo's security infrastructure and basically support two types of security: **Tuxedo application domain** and **link-level security**. The command-line utility scapasswordtool, provided by Tuxedo SALT, }is used to configure security for SALT's SCA client. This tool helps you to populate the encrypted password in the password.store file, but the user ID stays in text form. If the Tuxedo security is set with APP_PW or higher, an SCA component has to refer to it by searching in the password.store file.

Carry out the following steps to add/create a user ID / password (the password is not echoed on the screen):

1. Prompt> Enter scapasswordtool -i userID -a
2. Prompt> Enter password: password
3. Prompt> Confirm password: password

Run the following command to delete a password (user ID and password):

Prompt> scapasswordtool -i userID -d

In the previous section, we have briefly discussed all the different types of SCA-client and server-related configurations and security modules. For more detailed information, please refer to the following URL:

http://docs.oracle.com/cd/E15261_01/salt/docs11gr1/admin/config.html#wp1095401

Configuring the service contract discovery

The internal service of the TMMETADATA server gets the service contract information from the server that provides the service.

The TMMETADATA server's job is to produce a service contract by summarizing the collected data. This information is stored in the metadata repository. SALT uses the tmscd command to control the service contract runtime collection. The generated service's contract information contains the service name, request buffer information, and response buffer information, as well as the error buffer information if there is a failure. The collected service contract information is discarded if it fails to send information to the TMMETADATA server.

Configuring the SALT WS-TX support

This is to support a transaction for SALT components—inbound or outbound. Configuring the TLOG device for GWWS is the most important task, and it is similar to the way you create a TLOG file. The TLOGDevice element is added to the SALTDEPLOY file, and you will be sharing the same TLOG device for all GWWSs. Please refer to the format of this file, which we have discussed earlier. When Tuxedo is the coordinator (outbound direction) of a transaction, the GWWS system server permits either Volatile 2PC or Durable 2PC registration requests and handles them accordingly. To configure the maximum number of transactions, you can use MaxTran to configure the size of the internal transaction; the default is MAXGTT.

In this section, we have briefly discussed the configuration of SALT components; for example, the service metadata repository, the UBBCONFIG file, the GWWS server, SCA components (client and servers), and some examples of property files for more clarity.

Administration of SALT

In the previous section, we have seen the various tools and utilities to configure the SALT components; you may need to use these tools for administering and monitoring SALT. We have discussed most of the tasks involved in monitoring the service metadata repository. We have also discussed the service-deployment model, various SCA components, and GWWS during configuration. In the next section, we will briefly discuss some of the other tools and utilities that are going to serve this purpose with some tuning recommendations.

GWWS administration

The GWWS server is one of the most important components of SALT, and there are various tasks involved with it for administration purposes. We will discuss them in brief in this section.

Tuning the GWWS server

Some of the parameters of the GWWS property file should be looked at more carefully for tuning purposes. We are going to pick up a couple of them for our discussion. The following is an example of the properties file:

```
<Deployment ..>
  <WSGateway>
    <GWInstance id="MyGWWS">
      .......
      <Properties>
        <Property name="thread_pool_size" value="30"/>
        <Property name="max_content_length" value="2M"/>
        <Property name="timeout" value="700"/>
      </Properties>
    </GWInstance>
  </WSGateway>
</ Deployment>
```

Thread pool size

The GWWS server uses a thread pool working model to maximize the performance in a multiprocessor server environment. The default for the thread_pool_size parameter is 16, but you need to conduct a usage analysis to tune this parameter for large concurrent clients.

Network timeout control

The timeout parameter is used to set the network timeout value in the configuration file. The default timeout value is 300 seconds, but you should use it or tune it accordingly.

Maximum content length control

The max_content_length parameter is used to define the buffer size for an incoming HTTP message a client can send; by default (zero), there is no limit.

Benefits of multiple GWWS instances

To avoid bottlenecks due to network or low CPU resources, you may like to configure multiple GWWS instances and deploy them with the same web service binding on a distributed Tuxedo environment, which will help you boost application performance.

To tune your application, conduct a typical usage analysis so that you get a better estimate, for example, of the number of concurrent clients, the maximum message size being used or you want to control, and how timeout is working for the clients, and then set the parameters accordingly. If you need more throughputs even after this kind of activity, you may need to consider multiple GWWS servers to boost performance.

Monitoring the GWWS server

The command-line option wsadmin, which we have listed above, is the monitoring tool for the GWWS server. Both the TUXCONFIG and SALTCONFIG environment variables need to be set first and then you can execute wsadmin. You can run this command in either the active or the inactive mode. Here, we will discuss the various options (subcommands) you can use for monitoring purposes:

* gwstats: This shows various administrative data of a GWWS server on its services or instance
* configstats: This displays the configuration information
* default: This specifies the default -i option
* printtrans: This prints the transaction information for the GWWS instance
* verbose: This switches the verbose mode on/off
* quit: This is used to exit a program

Browsing to the WSDL document from the GWWS server

The WSDL gets created automatically by the GWWS server for each deployed inbound native WSDF. This WSDL can be downloaded from any of the HTTP/S listening endpoints via HTTP GET. You can use the following URL to browse the WSDL document:

```
http(s)://<host>:<port>/wsdl[? [id=<Value>] [&mappolicy=<Value>]
[&toolkit=<Value>]]
```

The following are the attributes of the previous URL:

- `id`: This specifies the native WSDF name for the WSDL.
- `mappolicy`: There are three options for this: `pack`, `raw`, and `mtom`.
- `toolkit`: There are two options for this: `wls` and `axis`. You can use these options only when you are using the `raw` type of `mappolicy`. SALT supports the WebLogic server (`wls`) and `axis` for SOAP with attachments; the default value is `wls`.

In the previous section, we have discussed how to administrate, tune, and monitor the GWWS server using various command-line utilities.

Administrating the SCA components

In this section, we will discuss how to administrate and monitor Tuxedo's SCA components. From the administrator's point of view, we can turn on the trace for SCA server/client and check them. For monitoring, we can use the command-line utility. Let us discuss these options briefly.

Tracing the SCA ATMI server and client

Tuxedo provides the tracing capability through the `tmtrace()` function, and it can be used for SCA ATMI servers and clients. All the messages are logged in the ULOG file as you set the TMTRACE environment variable, `TMTRACE=atmi:ulog`.

There are two environment variables for SCA runtime and reference binding and tracing, which can be used for Tuxedo server builds using `buildscaserver` and SCA client builds using `buildscaclient`:

- `SCACPP_LOGGING`: This numerical value is used to define the number of trace messages produced
- `SCACPP_ULOG`: You need to set the value to `yes` to send the trace messages to the ULOG file

For the SCA JTMI client, if you set the `$APPDIR` variable or the `com.oracle.jatmi.APPDIR` Java property is specified, you will see multiple logfiles (for example, `jatmi<numeric>.log`) under `$APPDIR`. By default, there will be 10 logfiles with the maximum size of 1 MB, and files are overwritten as you start the application.

Monitoring the SCA servers

The command-line utility `scaadmin` is to monitor the SCA servers, and it shows various service-related information and enables administrative tasks. You must set the `TUXCONFIG` environment variable accordingly as you run this utility. Here we will discuss the various options (subcommands) for `scaadmin`, which can be used for monitoring purposes:

- `default`: This sets the machine name, group name, server ID, or server name to default.
- `reload`: This dynamically reloads the SCA components hosted in a Tuxedo server. There are some limitations with some OSs for reloading.
- `printstats`: This displays the list of services within the Tuxedo environment, as well as the related methods, number of queries, and status.
- `verbose`: This is used to turn on the verbose mode.
- `echo`: This is used to echo the input on/off.
- `quit`: This is used to exit a session.

In this section, we have discussed most of the administrative tasks that should be performed in conjunction with tasks involved with the SALT configuration. We have also briefly brought up tuning issues and the various aspects of it.

SALT programming

SALT programming involves mainly two areas, namely **web services programming** and **SCA programming**, which are very much standard programing practices today. In this section, I will briefly introduce the programming paradigms for SALT, but I do not intend to go into the details, as we do want to cover how to do web service / SCA programing in this small book. Most of the SALT-related APIs are listed in the table in one of the previous sections of this chapter; we will be using them along with our web service / SCA programming knowledge.

Web services programming

As we have previously discussed, SALT provides bi-directional communication between the Tuxedo applications and web-service-based applications, and any existing Tuxedo services can be easily exposed as a web services without much coding. SALT helps you create a WSDL file that describes the Tuxedo web service contract so that any standard web service client can call or access Tuxedo services.

Invoking Tuxedo services (inbound) through SALT

As we have seen, the SALT components are configurable and we do not need to do too much of coding; it also helps you expose Tuxedo services as standard web services. So, a client needs to utilize the SALT's WSDL file to build a web service client program.

The following steps will help you develop a web service client program:

1. Create a WSDL file.
2. Create a client stub using the web-service client-side toolkit that parses the WSDL.
3. Develop a client application that can call a SALT web service utilizing the functions defined in the client stub.
4. Compile the application. You are now ready to run your client application.

Invoking external web services (outbound) through SALT

One of the features of SALT is to allow you to import external web services into Tuxedo domains. The conversion utility, `wsdlcvt`, should be used on WSDL in such a way that it translates each operation(s) specified in this file into a SALT proxy service. The translated SALT's proxy service can be invoked directly through the standard Tuxedo ATMI functions. These service calls are routed through the GWWS server. The request is translated from Tuxedo-type buffers into the SOAP message and then sent to the corresponding external web service. The response from an external web service is translated into Tuxedo-type buffers and returned to the Tuxedo application. Like any other Tuxedo development, you can use `tperrno` in case a call returns with an error; the GWWS server sets it accordingly. This enables you to detect and handle the SALT proxy service call's error status.

SCA programming

As we have seen in the first section, the SCA components use ATMI binding to run on a Tuxedo environment. The ATMI binding is built to set the communication paradigms between the SCA components and Tuxedo clients or servers. The runtime checks are encapsulated in an exception defined in a header (`tuxsca.h`) provided with the ATMI binding. This exception (`ATMIBindingException`) is derived from `ServiceRuntimeException` and thrown back to the caller. SALT's SCA programming utilities are listed in the first section of this chapter. You can build a client or server using the SCA components with these utilities.

SCA client programming

The following steps are needed to build an SCA client:

1. Set up the client directory structure to define the physical representation of an application; refer to the `root.composite` file.

2. Create the client application using a single API.

3. Compose the SCDL descriptor to create a link between the local and the actual component.

4. Build the client executable using `buildscaclient`.

5. Execute the client while making sure that the `APPDIR` and `SCA_COMPONENT` variables are set.

SCA component server programming

The following steps are required for developing an SCA component program:

1. Set up the component directory to define the physical representation of the application.

2. Develop the component implementation.

3. Compose the SCDL descriptor to define the binding between actual components and local implementation.

4. Compile and link the components using `buildscacomponent`.

5. Build the Tuxedo server host using `buildscaserver`.

SCA transactions

The ATMI binding schema supports SCA transaction policies by using the `/binding.atmi/@requires` attribute and the three transaction values `Not Specified`, `suspendsTransaction`, and `PropagatesTransaction`.

The various important areas in SCA programming that developers would be interested in are Python and Ruby scripts and integration with Tuxedo SALT for more development advantage; for example, no compilation, dynamic data typing, and garbage collection. SALT provides a set of APIs to perform SCA calls from the Python or Ruby client, and language extensions to call Python or Ruby components.

SALT programming is a huge topic and can have different aspects; for more information, refer to the program guide under the Oracle site:

`http://docs.oracle.com/cd/E15261_01/salt/docs11gr1/prog/index.html`

Also, there are some good examples provided by Oracle on the following site:

`http://docs.oracle.com/cd/E15261_01/salt/docs11gr1/samples/index.html`

Summary

Tuxedo provides many ways to connect with other SOA platforms and environments. As one of the original SOA platforms, SALT was introduced to make the Tuxedo platform more adaptable and extendable to the SOA world. By providing support for the SCA, SALT allows customers to quickly develop and compose SOA-based applications running on the most robust infrastructure in the industry. We have discussed how to configure and administrate various SALT components in this chapter. One important characteristic of SCA is the outlining of a new software design model, which has been picked up by IT community very well today. However, it is a huge topic and I do not intend to cover it in this book.

5
Oracle Tuxedo Joining the Exalogic Family

We have discussed how SALT helps us to integrate Tuxedo with the SOA environment; similarly, we will discuss how Exalogic extends a Tuxedo service into the cloud environment in this chapter. To start, we will briefly discuss the Exalogic machines and their architectural components and as well as benefits they bring to any IT organization. We will then move on to the installation of Tuxedo on an Exalogic machine. Finally, we will cover the most important part of this section: configuration of Tuxedo on an Exalogic machine. In the end, we will see how to run Tuxedo on Exalogic and some supporting tools to use for better usage.

What is Exalogic?

Exalogic is hardware and software engineered together to provide extreme performance for Java applications and all other enterprise applications. Exalogic uses the **InfiniBand** fabric to connect internal hardware such as processors, storage, memory, and external network interfaces inside the Exalogic machine, which works like one unified big and powerful computing device. What this means to us is that Exalogic is a machine where hardware, operation systems, networking, middleware, and applications are optimized under one umbrella to give you the best performance and stability. You should consider Exalogic as the foundation for your cloud environment where **Exabus**, a performance-boosting hardware; firmware; and software work together. Exabus eliminates I/O bottlenecks, which is ideal for cloud or application clustering. This is designed for virtualization.

The protocol bridging chipset for Ethernet network virtualization is unique to Exalogic. According to Oracle, Tuxedo gives 80 to 400 percent improvement and 8 times faster response time on an Exalogic machine.

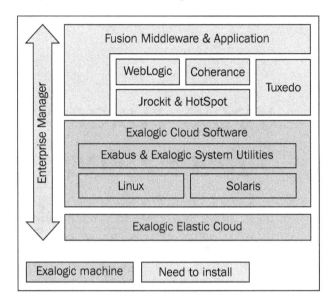

An Exalogic machine is built with Sun Fire X4170 M2 servers and the very high-speed Sun ZFS storage, and uses InfiniBand (switched-fabric communications link) and Ethernet networking components. It has four varieties: full rack with 32 nodes (Sun Fire X4170 M2), half rack with 16 nodes, quarter rack with 8 nodes, and eighth rack with 4 nodes.

Tuxedo installation on an Exalogic machine

The installation procedure of Tuxedo on an Exalogic machine is very similar to any other Unix- or Linux-based system. You need to make sure your Exalogic machine is commissioned, which includes networking configurations, IP address assignments, and setting up the storage. Please refer to the *Initial Configuration of an Exalogic Machine Using Oracle OneCommand* section in the Oracle Exalogic machine owners guide.

You need to pick the Oracle Tuxedo home directory; the recommendation is to install Oracle Tuxedo in one of the shares on Sun ZFS storage appliance locations so that you can run Oracle Tuxedo on any Exalogic node by having only one copy of Tuxedo executable.

You need to log in as a Tuxedo administrator and go to the installer directory where you downloaded it. The installation is very self-explanatory and simple. Please run the following command:

```
Prompt> sh./tuxedo111130_64_Linux_01_x86.bin-i console
```

You will be given options; pick a number to proceed with the installation of Tuxedo on an Exalogic machine.

```
Pick 1 for Local screen
Pick 1 for full install
Pick 1 for Oracle Home
Enter Oracle Home Directory (Shared file system)
Pick 2 for product directory
You may installed Samples by choosing "Y"
You need to press <Enter> as you see ready to install screen
Configure tlisten as installation finishes
SSL installation is not mandatory,  you need to setup LDAP if you like to
have SSL.
Your installation is complete and presses <Enter> to exit the installer.
```

So far, we have discussed what Exalogic is and how to install Tuxedo on it. The installation is very simple as long as you have commissioned the Exalogic machine properly.

Tuxedo configuration and runtime

We know how to configure various Tuxedo components quite well by now, so in this section we will discuss only the configuration relating to an Exalogic machine.

The UBBCONFIG file

In this section, we will discuss all the configuration related tasks using the UBBCONFIG file. We will be introduced to some more parameters in the UBBCONFIG file and some environment variables that need to be set for running Tuxedo on an Exalogic box. In MP mode, communication between two nodes is done through a bridge, but in Exalogic's cross-node, communication can be leveraged using **remote direct memory access (RDMA)**. You need to specify RDMA with option values in the MACHINES section; there are four options, which are as follows:

- RDMADAEMONIP: This is the IP (IPoIB) address, but it is not an Ethernet-based IP address, and the Msgq_daemon process is bound with it. You need to configure a one-to-one configuration for Msgq_daemon and the logical machine.

- DMADAEMONPORT: This is a listener port for the Msgq_daemon listener process.

- RDMAQSIZE: This is the queue (EMSQ) size; it's default value is 65,536 bytes if not defined in the UBBCONFIG file.

- RDMAQENTRIES: This is the entry number for a queue (EMSQ), which is the maximum number of messages in that queue.

Also, under the *RESOURCES section, you need to set the following:

- For the MODEL parameter – MP (for SHM mode, you need not use RDMA)
- For the OPTIONS parameter – LAN, EXALOGIC, and RDMA

Please make sure that the following things are checked and configured according to the guidelines mentioned:

- The shared directory for all Exalogic nodes needs to be enabled to leverage the RDMA feature. You need to make sure that the access permissions are properly set for it. The default name is /u01/common/patches/tuxtmpfile; you can also set your own directory using the EXALOGIC_SHARED_PATH environment variable. Tuxedo uses this file for message transfers when the EMSQ queue is full or the message size exceeds the queue size.

- Users from different Exalogic nodes must have read, write, or execution permission to the shared APPDIR variable, as it is shared by all nodes.

- Please set a different path for TUXCONFIG for each node.

- Please set a different path for ULOGPFX for each node.

- You need to set the `/etc/securitylimits.conf` parameter with the following values:

```
memlock   [Msgq_daemon shared memory size] * 2 + MAXACCESSERS *
14000(KB)
hard memlock 1853030
soft memlock 1853030
```

So, there are not too many changes to make in your UBBCONFIG file when compared to the normal Tuxedo configuration. I put in the `/etc/securitylimits` parameters and the EXALOGIC_SHARED_PATH environment variable as I want to make sure that we do all the basic things right before we bring up Tuxedo on an Exalogic box.

Tuxedo Socket Direct Protocol support

The **Socket Direct Protocol (SDP)** feature enables Tuxedo components using BSD socket APIs that can leverage the advantages of the SDP network protocol provided by Exalogic. This feature is high-bandwidth, low-latency, and needs reduced CPU involvement. To enable SDP in Tuxedo, you must specify EXALOGIC for OPTIONS in the *RESOURCE section, which we have seen earlier, and set the relevant configuration in the UBBCONFIG file or the DMCONFIG (in the DOMAIN configuration) file. We will now show you how to use SDP for the MP mode, DOMAIN, WSL and WS Client, and JSL and WTC.

The MP mode

In the MP mode, both master and slave machines are inside the IB cluster, so only consider that SDP and IPoIB are being used inside the IB cluster; in the bootstrap phase, `tmboot`, `tlisten`, `bsbridge`, and `bridge` are using socket APIs to communicate with each other.

To configure SDP in the MP mode, you need to add `sdp:` as a prefix to the network address, and the network address the must be an IPoIB address. You can refer to the following example:

```
*NETWORK
Node1              NADDR="sdp://IB_IP: 9933"
                   NLSADDR="sdp://IB_IP: 3355"
Node2              NADDR="sdp://IB_IP: 9933"
                   NLSADDR="sdp://IB_IP: 3355"
```

To start `tlisten`, you can use Prompt> `tlisten  -d /dev/tcp -l sdp://IB_IP: 3355`.

To configure IPoIB in the MP mode, use the IPoIB address as the network address.

```
*NETWORK
Node1          NADDR="//IB_IP: 9933"
               NLSADDR="//IB_IP: 3355"
Node2          NADDR="//IB_IP: 9933"
               NLSADDR="//IB_IP: 3355"
```

To start `tlisten`, you can use `Prompt> tlisten  -d /dev/tcp  -l //IB_IP: 3355`.

GWTDOMAIN

Functionally, if you look at the domain architecture, you may find that the GWTDOMAIN server acts as both server and client. As a server, it will listen on a configured IP address and port number in the DMCONFIG file to accept a connection request from another GWTDOMAIN. As a client, it will initiate a connection request to another GWTDOMAIN by the policy configured in the DMCONFIG file. It is more useful to use an explicit IP address when configuring GWTDOMAIN in the DMCONFIG file, though you can configure it with a hostname.

Normally, every Exalogic node has at least two types of network interface: an IB interface and an Ethernet interface. So, to configure GWTDOMAIN, you take the IB interface to bind with the IP address IB_IP, and the Ethernet interface to bind with IP address ETH_IP. We have the following four examples listed to show you how to configure GWTDOMAIN in the DMCONFIG file to use SDP or IPoIB as server and client respectively in an Exalogic environment.

Configuring GWTDOMAIN to listen on SDP

To configure the gateway domain to listen to SDP, you need to add NWADDR with a port number as shown in the following example:

```
*DM_LOCAL
Node1          GWGRP=DOMGRP
               TYPE=TDOMAIN
*DM_TDOMAIN
               Node1    NWADDR="sdp://IB_IP: 27766"
```

Configuring GWTDOMAIN to connect using SDP

To configure the gateway domain to connect to SDP, you need to add NWADDR with a port number as shown in the following example:

```
*DM_LOCAL
Node1          GWGRP=DOMGRP
               TYPE=TDOMAIN
```

```
*DM_REMOTE
Node2                    TYPE=TDOMAIN
                         DOMAINID="EXALOGIC_Node2"
*DM_TDOMAIN

                 Node2   NWADDR="sdp://IB_IP: 27766"
```

Configuring GWTDOMAIN to listen on IPoIB

To configure the gateway domain to listen to IPoIB, you need to add NWADDR with a port number as shown in the following example:

```
*DM_LOCAL
Node2                    GWGRP=DOMGRP
                         TYPE=TDOMAIN
*DM_TDOMAIN
 Node2                   NWADDR="//IB_IP: 27766"
```

Configuring GWTDOMAIN to connect using IPoIB

To configure the gateway domain to connect through IPoIB, you need to add NWADDR with a port number as shown in the following example:

```
*DM_LOCAL
Node2                    GWGRP=DOMGRP
                         TYPE=TDOMAIN
*DM_REMOTE
Node3                    TYPE=TDOMAIN
                         DOMAINID="EXALOGIC_ Node3"
*DM_TDOMAIN
Node3                    NWADDR="//IB_IP: 27766"
```

The workstation listener (WSL)

To configure WSL on SDP or IpoIB, you need to use the following option in the DMCONFIG file:

- **WSL listening on SDP** – Refer to the following example on using the WSL configuration using SDP:

```
*SERVERS
DEFAULT:    CLOPT="-A"
WSL         SRVGRP=WSGRP   SRVID=1001
            CLOPT="-A -- -n sdp://IB_IP: 11101 -m1 -M10 -x1"
```

- **WSL listening on IPoIB** – Refer to the following example on using the WSL configuration using IPoIB:

```
*SERVERS
DEFAULT:      CLOPT="-A"
WSL           SRVGRP=WSGRP   SRVID=1001
              CLOPT="-A -- -n  //IB_IP: 11101 -m1 -M10 -x1"
```

The workstation (/WS) client

For the workstation (/WS) client, you need to set the WSNADDR environment variable in the following ways:

- **SDP**: export WSNADDR=sdp://IB_IP:1001

- **IpoIB**: export WSNADDR=//IB_IP:1001

The jolt service listener (JSL)

The JSL setup is similar to WSL; you need to use the following option in the DMCONFIG file:

- **JSL listening on SDP** – Refer to the following example on working with the JSL configuration using SDP:

```
*SERVERS
DEFAULT:    CLOPT="-A"
JSL         SRVGRP=WSGRP SRVID=1001
            CLOPT="-A -- -n sdp: //IB_IP: 11101 -m1 -M10 -x1"
```

- **JSL listening on IPoIB** – Refer to the following example on working with the JSL configuration using IPoIB:

```
*SERVERS
DEFAULT:      CLOPT="-A"
JSL           SRVGRP=WSGRP SRVID=1001
              CLOPT="-A -- -n //IB_IP: 11101 -m1 -M10 -x1"
```

The WebLogic Tuxedo connector (WTC)

You need to do the following two steps to enable an SDP connection between the WTC and Tuxedo:

1. Specify the NWADDR value of the WTC service local/remote access points as follows:

```
sdp://IB_IP:port
```

It is the same as the GWTDOMAIN's `NWADDR` configuration in the `DMCONFIG` file.

2. You need to put an additional Java option in the WLS start-up command as follows:

```
-Djava.net.preferIPv4Stack=true        java command-line
```

Databases

There is nothing special you need to do to use the database or XA interface, as this standard is widely supported on all the major database vendor products. You may want to use SDP for Oracle database invocations, but again, you don't need to perform anything special in a Tuxedo application. You do however need to configure the database to support InfiniBand. You can set the two parameters in `/etc/modprobe.conf` on the server node for better performance (for example, `options ib_sdp sdp_zcopy_thresh=0  recv_poll=0`). It's default value is 64 KB, but the recommendation is to set it with zero.

The EXALOGIC_MSGQ_CACHE_SIZE variable

The `EXALOGIC_MSGQ_CACHE_SIZE` environment variable can be used to improve the performance of the Tuxedo application. This value can be set between 32 and 2,048. One thing to notice is that increasing the number can improve Tuxedo's performance, but `Msgq_daemon` consumes more shared memory. So, setting this environment variable will help you to get better performance during the process of sending multiple messages to many queues.

Please read the following recommendation from Oracle:

If there are 40 remote Oracle Tuxedo servers providing the same service and clients call the service 100 times, setting EXALOGIC_MSGQ_CACHE_SIZE to a value equal to or greater than 40 on the client improves performance.

If there are 50 WSHs, and each WSH receives response messages from the same remote server, setting EXALOGIC_MSGQ_CACHE_SIZE to a value equal to or greater than 50 on the server environment improves performance.

Running Oracle Tuxedo

In this section, we will discuss how to start and stop Tuxedo and the tools that are available for various administrative purposes. There are some differences in running Tuxedo on a non-Exalogic platform with RDMA features. The `tux_msgq_monitor` function must be started before booting a Tuxedo application.

Start/stop tux_msgq_monitor

As we just discussed, tux_msgq_monitor should be started before booting the Oracle Tuxedo application. The tux_msgq_monitor function is responsible for starting Msgq_daemon and checking its running status. Before starting tux_msgq_monitor, ensure that the environment variables TUXCONFIG, LD_LIBRARY_PATH, and TUXDIR are properly set. If Msgq_daemon terminates abnormally for some reason or other, it restarts using tux_msgq_monitor. One monitor can only serve one Oracle Tuxedo application on one logical machine.

Start tux_msgq_monitor

The following command is an example to start tux_msgq_monitor:

```
Prompt> tux_msgq_monitor  -i <IPoIB>  -d <port#>  -M <size> -K < key>
```

The following are the attributes of this command:

- -i – This IPoIB address should be equal to the RDMADAEMONIP parameter in in the UBBCONFIG file.

- -d – This port number should be the same number as that mentioned in RDMADAEMONPORT in the UBBCONFIG file.

- -M – The shared memory gets allocated as you start Msgq_daemon. So, it is very important for you to estimate the size of the shared memory. You can get the memory size by using tmloadcf -c ubb.

- -K – This is the key number to access the shared memory by Msgq_daemon.

When tux_msgq_monitor is running, you should check and make sure that the tux_msgq_monitor and Msgq_daemon processes are running. After starting tux_msgq_monitor successfully, you can boot the Tuxedo application.

You can also use a shell script that helps you start all the processes in the master node, that is, tux_msgq_monitor and a Tuxedo application. Please make sure that the environment variables TUXCONFIG, LD_LIBRARY_PATH, and APPDIR are set properly before you run this command. So, to be very specific, the following script starts up tux_msgq_monitor, executes tmboot to start the Oracle Tuxedo application, and starts tlisten if the option -l is specified:

```
Prompt> tmboot.sh  -i daemon_ip -d daemon_port -M shm_size -K shm_key
[-l nlsaddr]
```

On the slave node, you can run the following command to start the tux_msgq_monitor and tlisten functions:

```
Prompt> tlisten_start.sh  -l nlsaddr -i daemon_ip -d daemon_port -M shm_size -K shm_key
```

On an MP mode configuration, you need to run the commands in the following order:

```
Prompt> tmlisten_start.sh          on all the slave nodes
Prompt> tmboot.sh                  on the master node
```

Stop tux_msgq_monitor

You need to use the kill command while using the -9 option with pid of tux_msgq_monitor; use ipcrm to clear the IPC resources.

```
Prompt> kill -9 "pid of Msgq_daemon"
Prompt> ipcrm - m "shmid"
```

Like the start-up shell script, you can also run a shutdown command on the master node to stop both the Tuxedo application and tux_msgq_monitor.

```
Prompt> tmshut.sh
```

On the slave node, you can run the following command:

```
Prompt> tlisten_stop.sh
```

To shut down all the processes on an MP mode configuration, you need to run the commands in the following order:

```
Prompt> tmshut.sh                  on the master node.
Prompt> tmlisten_stop.sh           on all the slave nodes.
```

So, this basically concludes all the relevant topics we intended to cover regarding Tuxedo on an Exalogic machine. We discussed the Exalogic machine and its various benefits and components, how to install Tuxedo on it and then configure it, and finally how to start and stop a Tuxedo application.

Summary

We have discussed the importance of SOA and cloud-based elastic capacity for enterprise IT organizations to provide more demanding performance and reliability to meet business requirements and agility. It is not so easy to build custom, special-purpose systems for different applications, as it would be very complex, time consuming, and expensive. The Exalogic elastic cloud is considered to be one of the first integrated middleware machines; it far surpasses the alternatives and provides enterprises with the best possible foundation for running applications. The good news for Tuxedo users is that it runs on Exalogic while leveraging all of Exalogic's features to the fullest, and it gives much better results on performance, reliability, and scalability for IT.

In this book, we have covered how to install, configure, and develop a Tuxedo application and its various components in brief. To do this, we have basically covered the last 30 years of client/server technology in 90 pages! We started with the basics of client/server architecture, where I depicted all the components in one diagram to show how Tuxedo does it seamlessly. It's been a great platform to build your applications for the last 20 years, and it seems it is true for the present too! The idea of having a service or business services was introduced by Tuxedo from its initial days. We have seen how we can design a Tuxedo application in a loosely coupled manner in a distributed environment that is also very transparent in nature. We have discussed how to make a Tuxedo application scalable and available, and which maximizes resource utilization by using its load-balancing algorithm. We have seen the richness of Tuxedo APIs, which are proven, and you can build a mission-critical application easily by using them. We have also discussed how to use Tuxedo in your SOA environment using its SALT plugins. Service Components Architecture (SCA) is the new buzzword in today's BPEL world, and Tuxedo is up there to be used as a component that is a part of a composite, or vice versa. Last but not least, Tuxedo is in the cloud— a Tuxedo application running on an Exalogic platform. You need to do very few things to run Tuxedo on an Exalogic box; you only have to change some common parameters in UBBCONFIG and DMCONFIG. So, it seems Tuxedo is going to be here for a long time with it's adaptability on the technology front. I am very proud as a Tuxedo user, and it is very satisfying for me that I could share some of my experience with you in this book. It is a small book, but I have tried to include the most important aspects of Tuxedo; I hope this book helps you to build a foundation on Tuxedo and that you will carry it forward from here.

Index

P

paradigms, for client/server communication
  conversational 77, 87
  event-based communication 89, 90
  publish and subscribe (Pub-sub) 77
  Queues (Tuxedo /Q) 87-89
  queuing 77
  request/reply 87
  request/response 77
PATH variable 21
performance-related monitoring tasks, TSAM 51, 52
printqueue [qaddress] command 43

Q

qmadmin command 40, 62, 63
QMCONFIG variable 22

R

RDMADAEMONIP option 128
RDMADAEMONPORT option 128
RDMAQENTRIES option 128
RDMAQSIZE option 128
remote direct memory access (RDMA) 128
RESOURCES section
  about 26
  parameters 26, 27
rex command 40
ROUTING section
  about 34
  parameters 34

S

SALT
  about 13, 95, 98, 125
  administering 116
  console-based installation 100
  external web services, invoking through 121
  GUI-based installation 99
  silent-mode installation 100
  Tuxedo services, invoking through 121

SALT application
  configuring 101
SALT configuration
  compiling 113
SALTDEPLOY file
  about 111
  creating 112, 113
SALT gateway (GWWS) 97
SALT programming 120
SALT WS-TX support
  configuring 116
SCA 7, 97
scaadmin function 103
SCA ATMI client
  configuring 113
  tracing 119
SCA ATMI server
  configuring 115
  tracing 119
SCA client programming 122
SCA client security
  configuring 115
SCA components
  administering 119
  configuring 113
SCA component server programming 122
SCAHOST function 104
SCA JATMI client
  configuring 114
scapasswordtool function 104, 115
SCA programming 120, 121
SCA servers
  monitoring 120
scastructc32 function 104
scastructc function 104
scastructdis32 function 104
scastructdis function 104
SCA transactions 122, 123
scatuxgen function 104
SCA web service client
  configuring 114
SCA web service server
  configuring 115
SCA workstation client
  configuring 114
sections, UBBCONFIG file
  about 25

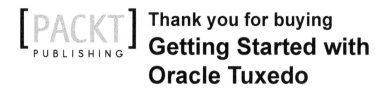
Thank you for buying
**Getting Started with
Oracle Tuxedo**

About Packt Publishing

Packt, pronounced 'packed', published its first book "*Mastering phpMyAdmin for Effective MySQL Management*" in April 2004 and subsequently continued to specialize in publishing highly focused books on specific technologies and solutions.

Our books and publications share the experiences of your fellow IT professionals in adapting and customizing today's systems, applications, and frameworks. Our solution based books give you the knowledge and power to customize the software and technologies you're using to get the job done. Packt books are more specific and less general than the IT books you have seen in the past. Our unique business model allows us to bring you more focused information, giving you more of what you need to know, and less of what you don't.

Packt is a modern, yet unique publishing company, which focuses on producing quality, cutting-edge books for communities of developers, administrators, and newbies alike. For more information, please visit our website: www.packtpub.com.

Writing for Packt

We welcome all inquiries from people who are interested in authoring. Book proposals should be sent to author@packtpub.com. If your book idea is still at an early stage and you would like to discuss it first before writing a formal book proposal, contact us; one of our commissioning editors will get in touch with you.

We're not just looking for published authors; if you have strong technical skills but no writing experience, our experienced editors can help you develop a writing career, or simply get some additional reward for your expertise.

Getting Started with Oracle Data Integrator 11g: A Hands-On Tutorial

Combine high volume data movement, complex transformations and real-time data integration with the robust capabilities of ODI in this practical guide

Foreword by Alok Pareek
Vice President, Data Integration Product Management at Oracle

Peter C. Boyd-Bowman   Christophe Dupupet
Denis Gray   David Hecksel
Julien Testut   Bernard Wheeler

Getting Started with Oracle Data Integrator 11g: A Hands-On Tutorial

ISBN: 978-1-84968-068-4   Paperback: 384 pages

Combine high volume data movement, complex transformations and real-time data integration with the robust capabilities of ODI in this practical guide

1. Discover the comprehensive and sophisticated orchestration of data integration tasks made possible with ODI, including monitoring and error-management

2. Get to grips with the product architecture and building data integration processes with technologies including Oracle, Microsoft SQL Server and XML files

3. A comprehensive tutorial packed with tips, images and best practices

Oracle Advanced PL/SQL Developer Professional Guide

Master advanced PL/SQL concepts along with plenty of example questions for 1Z0-146 examination

Foreword by
Ronald Rood, Oracle ACE, Oracle DBA, OCM
Kamran Agayev A., Oracle ACE, Oracle DBA Expert

Saurabh K. Gupta

Oracle Advanced PL/SQL Developer Professional Guide

ISBN: 978-1-84968-722-5   Paperback: 440 pages

Master advanced PL/SQL concepts along with plenty of example questions for 1Z0-146 examination

1. Blitz the 1Z0-146 exam

2. Master the advanced features of PL/SQL to design and optimize code using real-time demonstrations

3. Efficiently design PL/SQL code with cursor design and subtypes

Please check **www.PacktPub.com** for information on our titles

**Oracle Business Intelligence
Enterprise Edition 11g:
A Hands-On Tutorial**

Leverage the latest Fusion Middleware Business Intelligence
offering with this action-packed implementation guide

Haroun Khan   Christian Screen
Adrian Ward   [PACKT] enterprise

Oracle Business Intelligence
Enterprise Edition 11g: A
Hands-On Tutorial

ISBN: 978-1-84968-566-5   Paperback:620 pages

Leverage the latest Fusion Middleware Business
Intelligence offering with this action-packed
implementation guide

1. Get to grips with the OBIEE 11g suite for
   analyzing and reporting on your business data

2. Immerse yourself in BI upgrading techniques,
   using Agents and the Action Framework and
   much more in this book and e-book

3. A practical, from the coalface tutorial, bursting
   with step by step instructions and real world
   case studies to help you implement the suite's
   powerful analytic capabilities

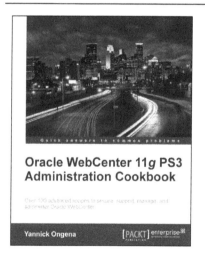

**Oracle WebCenter 11g PS3
Administration Cookbook**

Over 100 advanced recipes to secure, support, manage, and
administer Oracle WebCenter

Yannick Ongena   [PACKT] enterprise

Oracle WebCenter 11g PS3
Administration Cookbook

ISBN: 978-1-84968-228-2   Paperback: 348 pages

Over 100 advanced recipes to secure, support,
manage, and administer Oracle WebCenter

1. The only book and eBook in the market that
   focuses on administration tasks using the new
   features of WebCenter 11g PS3

2. Understand the use of Wiki and Discussion
   services to build collaborative portals

3. Full of illustrations, diagrams, and tips with
   clear step-by-step instructions and real-world
   examples

Please check **www.PacktPub.com** for information on our titles